CAPITAL PUNISHMENT

BOOK SOLD
NO LONGER R.H. P.L.
PROPERTY

RICHMOND HILL
PUBLIC LIBRARY

OCT 1 7 2011

RICHMOND GREEN
905-780-0711

CAPITAL PUNISHMENT

An Indictment by a Death-Row Survivor

BILLY WAYNE SINCLAIR
and JODIE SINCLAIR

Foreword by Sister Helen Prejean

Arcade Publishing
NEW YORK

RICHMOND HILL
PUBLIC LIBRARY

OCT 1 7 2011

RICHMOND GREEN
905-780-0711

Copyright © 2009, 2011 by Billy Wayne Sinclair and Jodie Sinclair
Foreword copyright © 2009, 2011 by Sister Helen Prejean

All Rights Reserved. No part of this book may be reproduced in any manner
without the express written consent of the publisher, except in the case of brief
excerpts in critical reviews or articles. All inquiries should be addressed to
Arcade Publishing, 307 West 36th Street, 11th Floor, New York, NY 10018.

Arcade Publishing books may be purchased in bulk at special discounts
for sales promotion, corporate gifts, fund-raising, or educational purposes.
Special editions can also be created to specifications. For details, contact the
Special Sales Department, Arcade Publishing, 307 West 36th Street, 11th
Floor, New York, NY 10018 or info@skyhorsepublishing.com.

Arcade Publishing® is a registered trademark of Skyhorse Publishing, Inc.®,
a Delaware corporation.

Visit our website at www.arcadepub.com.

10 9 8 7 6 5 4 3 2 1

Library of Congress Cataloging-in-Publication Data

Sinclair, Billy Wayne, 1945-
  Capital punishment : an indictment by a death-row survivor / Billy Wayne
Sinclair and Jodie Sinclair ; foreword by Sister Helen Prejean.
    p. cm.
  Originally published in 2009.
  ISBN 978-1-61145-034-7 (pbk. : alk. paper)
  1. Capital punishment--United States. 2. Sinclair, Billy Wayne, 1945- 3.
Death row inmates--United States. I. Sinclair, Jodie, 1938- II. Title.
  HV8699.U5S475 2011
  364.66092--dc22
                        2011001610

Printed in the United States of America

This book is dedicated to Richard Seaver,
an editor with the courage to publish the truth.

The man who opts for revenge should dig two graves.

—Chinese proverb

Contents

Foreword

Arguments against the death penalty expose capital punishment for what it is: revenge disguised as justice.

When there is a conviction in a capital case, the prosecutor appears before the jury arguing that it must impose the death penalty because the criminal poses a continuing threat to society. Billy Wayne Sinclair's life refutes that claim. It argues for a different perspective on individuals who have been convicted in capital cases.

His early life is similar to those of other death row inmates in many ways. He was repeatedly beaten as a small child by a brutal father who ultimately abandoned the family. He grew up in extreme poverty with a single mother in rural Louisiana. He dropped out of school in the tenth grade after pushing a school principal to the ground. In 1965, during a bungled robbery attempt when he was twenty years old, Billy killed a convenience store clerk with a wild shot intended to frighten him as he was chasing Billy across a parking lot in the dark.

A year later, a Baton Rouge judge sentenced him to die in Louisiana's electric chair. He spent five and a half years in solitary confinement on death row at the

Louisiana State Penitentiary at Angola. In 1972 the U.S. Supreme Court struck down the death penalty nationwide, and Billy was resentenced to life.

Today he is a hardworking paralegal for a criminal defense attorney in Houston. He has been married for twenty-seven years to the coauthor of this book, Jodie Sinclair, a former journalist. He is a national award–winning writer on prison issues, and he was a model inmate during his near half-century behind bars. There are no instances of violence in his prison record.

Billy Wayne Sinclair personifies the humanity of the condemned and their capacity to change. Clearly redemption is not limited to souls without sin.

Sister Helen Prejean

Preface

I served more than forty years in the Louisiana prison system for a murder I committed in 1965. Six of those years I spent on death row.

In April 1966, in a Baton Rouge courtroom, a judge spoke the words that shaped my life from that moment on: "Billy Wayne Sinclair, I hereby sentence you to death in the electric chair."

The sentence staggered me. I was only twenty-one years old, and I was condemned to die.

Granted, I had created the circumstances that condemned me to that death. I had tried to hold up a Baton Rouge convenience store, and, in a robbery gone wrong, I fired a wild shot in the direction of the store manager who was chasing me in the dark. The bullet nicked his aorta, and he bled to death on the sidewalk.

I grappled at first with the immediate implications of my death sentence. Nearly 3,000 volts of electricity would course through me for two minutes, cooking my brain, while my body convulsed against the chair's thick leather straps. I dealt with the horrifying prospect by denying it. I swallowed daily the tranquilizers that guards handed out to inmates on death row to keep them pacified, and then begged other inmates for their pills. Those pills kept me stoned for six months straight.

When I finally tired of my drug-induced stupor, I confronted my sentence head on. If the system intended to kill me, I wanted to learn everything about the monstrous sins it committed in carrying out the ultimate sentence. I read anything I could find about decapitation, hanging, death by firing squad, and electrocution. I studied the modes and methods of killing, like a scientist peering through a microscope at a deadly bacillus.[1] And for almost six years, I woke up every day to the possibility that guards might drag me from a death-house holding cell, strap me into the electric chair, and put me to death by one of the most gruesome forms of execution ever devised.

That the United States Supreme Court's decision saved me has not erased my fear of, or my fascination with, state-sanctioned murder. Every headline about the death penalty, every controversial court case, every DNA exoneration grabs my attention. I still study capital punishment—the emotional and social impact on the condemned, their families, their loved ones, the victims' families, and the general public. My death sentence will stay with me for the rest of my life.

I began writing about the death penalty on death row. My first article appeared in a religious pamphlet called *Power for Living*, earning me $35 for my account of a religious experience I had on death row. Publication

---

1. Appendix A gives a list, by no means comprehensive, of various execution methods used through history.

elated me. Death didn't have to silence me. I could live through writing. I pounded away feverishly in my cell — on a 1922 Underwood typewriter traded for a carton of cigarettes — documenting guards' abuses and the awful specter of death that twisted human lives into parodies of human experience.

Then, one hot June morning in 1972, the Supreme Court struck down the death sentence nationwide in *Furman v. Georgia*, ruling that it was being applied inequitably. There was no official announcement. Every man on the row, except those who had gone mad waiting to die, heard the news over the radio. The news stunned us, and we greeted it with silence. Suddenly, at age twenty-seven, I had a future. I could breathe beyond the moment. I stretched out on my prison bunk and immediately fell asleep, exhausted from years of dread.

Louisiana promptly resentenced me to life without parole and moved me into the general population at Angola in November 1972. I held a number of inmate jobs over the years, from stoop labor in the prison's fields, tending crops under the eyes of shotgun-toting guards on horseback, to a desk job clerking for the prison's food manager. But I never gave up writing. I contributed regular articles to two inmate publications at the prison, the *Angolite* and *Lifer* magazine, writing about a range of prison issues. And through it all I kept my study of capital punishment, kept collecting facts about the one sentence that cannot be reversed once it has been carried out.

In 1977 the prison's warden assigned me to the staff of the *Angolite*. I wrote full-time for the magazine for nearly ten years. My articles won a number of prestigious journalism awards, including the 1979 Robert Kennedy Special Journalism Award, the 1980 George Polk Award, the 1980 American Bar Association's Silver Gavel Award, and the 1981 Sidney Hillman Award.

Then I submitted stories about crime and prison life to newspapers, magazines, prison journals, literary journals, law journals, and law enforcement publications. *Police* magazine published my work, as did *Chief of Police* magazine. When readers discovered I was a prisoner, the editor expressed his personal regrets that my submissions could no longer be considered.

In 2000 my autobiography, *A Life in the Balance*, coauthored with my wife, Jodie, appeared. Then in 2004, noted lecturer and writer Paul Rogat Loeb invited me to write an article for an anthology on hope and courage in the face of adversity, called *The Impossible Will Take a Little While*. It included pieces by Vaclav Havel, Jim Hightower, Martin Luther King Jr., Nelson Mandela, Pablo Neruda, Desmond Tutu, Alice Walker, and Marian Wright Edelman, among others.

I am a journalist by trade, if not by training. Journalists report on issues and events — good and bad — that impact society. Capital punishment should be among them. It balances the rights of the condemned, the victims of crime, and society at large. We must continuously reevaluate fact and opinion in the face of the ultimate sentence.

When my wife and I began writing *A Life in the Balance*, we had a single goal: to tell the story of one man's prison experience in twentieth-century America as accurately as possible, devoid of a political agenda. This book is colored with our personal and political biases. To that, we readily confess. While the journalists in us objectively presented the facts about the death penalty, our feelings about capital punishment shaped both the content and direction of the chapters in this book. We hope you do not forget them.

Billy Wayne Sinclair and Jody Sinclair

1

The Justice Gene

Americans have been debating whether the death penalty is a just punishment since the colonies revolted against the oppressive, often brutal dictates of the English crown.

In *A History of American Law*, the first book to outline the development of American jurisprudence from colonial times to the late twentieth century, Lawrence Friedman writes of an era in which the young nation came into being: "The late eighteenth century . . . was a period in which intellectuals began to rethink the premises on which criminal law rested," arguing for "a more enlightened criminal law."

Americans enshrined this concept in the Bill of Rights, which protects the accused and saves criminals from "cruel and unusual punishment." But it does not outlaw capital punishment. The ultimate sentence remains on the books in a majority of states today despite attempts since the colonial period to abolish it.

The debate over capital punishment has raged back and forth since then, ebbing and flowing with public opinion and the tenor of the times. But America has never come close to banning it.

Why do Americans cling so tenaciously to a punishment that cannot be rescinded once it has been carried out — often in monstrous ways — even in cases where compelling evidence of innocence surfaces before an execution? Perhaps our frontier history with its urgent need to curb lawlessness across a vast wilderness has left us more attuned to a natural consequence of our evolution. Perhaps the answer lies in our genes.

Millions of years before recorded history, our small apelike ancestors stood up on their hind legs and began a struggle to survive on the African veldt, virtually defenseless in a vicious place for which they had abandoned the safety of the trees. In the fossil record over the long evolutionary march toward *Homo sapiens*, their bones and those of their descendants reveal the physical changes that resulted in us: upright creatures with bigger frames, longer bones, and larger brains.

But the fossil record reveals little about the thoughts and emotions that coursed through their brains as our ancestors made their long, gradual trek toward modern man. We must wonder, then, whence comes the common mindset that governs our behavior.

Science suggests that it evolved in a setting that demanded social cooperation for survival. Imagine a group of hominids. One of its members has eaten more than its fair share of the group's food. Now watch the group as a whole brutally assaulting the offender, possibly beating it to death. In a place and time where food was scarce and life itself was risked to gather it, the entire group might die of starvation if the behavior of the offender went unchecked. Such a scene resonates with us. We easily understand the need for this punishment.

On January 22, 2002, the *New York Times* ran an article by Natalie Angier, "The Urge to Punish Cheats: It Isn't Merely Vengeance," which said that "a willingness, even eagerness, to punish transgressors of the social compact is at least as important to the maintenance of social harmony as are regular displays of common human decency." Her article cited a study by two Swiss scientists, Dr. Ernst Fehr of the University of Zurich and Dr. Simon Gächter of the University of St. Gallen, the results of which had appeared in the January 10 edition of the journal *Nature*. The scientists' article, "Altruistic Punishment in Humans," suggested that the threat of punishment contributed significantly to the evolution of human civilization, as people "will seek to punish a cheat even when the punishment is costly to them and offers no material benefit."

"It's a very important force for establishing large-scale cooperation," Dr. Fehr explained to Angier in a telephone interview. "Every citizen is a little policeman in a sense. There are so many social norms that we follow almost unconsciously, and they are enforced by the moral outrage we expect if we were to violate them."

Even some extreme acts, Angier wrote, such as "torture, public stonings and lynchings, may all be examples of . . . altruistic behavior run amok."

Later that year, on July 23, Angier reported on a study that supports this idea. Cooperation — that is, altruistic behavior — makes areas of the brain associated with pleasurable activities light up under the watch of an MRI. When individuals who participated in a study at Emory University cooperated with each other during a complex lab experiment that involved brain imaging, the pleasure centers of their brains glowed with "quiet joy," as Angier described it in her *Times* article "Why We're So Nice: We're Wired to Cooperate."

During periods of cooperation, Angier reported, "the researchers found that . . . two broad areas of the brain were activated, both rich in neurons able to respond to dopamine, the brain chemical famed for its role in addictive behavior." Thus we are wired to cooperate.

We are also wired to exact revenge, it seems. In his 2004 article in the *New York Times*, "Payback Time: Why Revenge Tastes So Sweet," Benedict Carey quotes Dr. Joseph Henrich, an Emory University anthropologist, who says that some individuals "have an intrinsic taste for punishing others who violate a community's norms." Carey's article cites research that points to "a biological rooted sense of justice."

In a 2008 article for Reuters, "Bullies May Get a Kick Out of Seeing Others in Pain," Julie Steenhuysen reports that brain scans of "teens with a history of aggressive bullying behavior" suggest that "they may get pleasure from seeing someone else in pain."

Can we become addicted to punishing others because of the pleasure we feel when we execute criminals to protect the group? Is that sadism?

DEATH BY FIRING SQUAD

According to the Espy File (*Executions in the United States,*

4

1608–1987, by M. Watt Espy and John Ortiz Smylka), the first person executed in the United States was George Randall. He was killed by firing squad in Virginia in 1608 for the crime of espionage. Exactly four centuries later, the firing squad is still the most common method of execution in the world, used by some seventy countries to put people to death. Historically a "soldier's punishment," many considered the firing squad the most honorable form of execution. The Espy File estimates that 142 judicially ordered firing-squad executions took place in the United States between 1608 and 1987 (excluding the Civil War, when records were not kept of battlefield executions).

The last person put to death by firing squad in the United States was John Albert Taylor, a convicted child killer executed in Utah in 1996, the forty-ninth person executed by firing squad in that state. *Salt Lake Tribune* reporter Hal Schindler, who witnessed Taylor's execution and four others by firing squad, said it took only forty-five seconds for Warden Hank Galetka to place the hood over Taylor's head and step from the execution chamber before four .30-caliber bullets slammed into the condemned man's heart, killing him instantly. Proponents of the death penalty will no doubt call this quick death merciful. The speed and precision of Taylor's execution would seem to make death by firing squad the preferred mode of execution: better for the inmate and the squeamish. In addition to Utah, two others states, Oklahoma and Idaho, use the firing squad as an alternative method of execution.

A Utah firing squad consists of five volunteer police officers from the county in which the crime occurred. One of the squad's rifles is loaded with a blank. No member of the squad knows which rifle contains the blank. But there is reason to question Utah's claims about this procedure in at least one instance: the execution of Gary Gilmore on January 17, 1977. In his autobiography, *Shot in the Heart*, Mikal Gilmore said that when he examined the shirt worn by his brother during the execution, it had five bullet holes. All five members of the firing squad fired live rounds into Gary Gilmore. There was no blank.

Utah abolished death by firing squad in 2004 and now uses lethal injection to kill its inmates. But the law was not retroactive, so inmates with a death sentence imposed before that date can choose between firing squad and lethal injection. An inmate who chooses the firing squad sits in a specially designed chair in which guards restrain his or her arms, legs, and chest. The head is loosely confined so that it remains upright.

The condemned inmate wears a dark blue outfit with a white cloth circle attached by Velcro over the heart. Sandbags behind the chair catch the four — or five — bullets and prevent ricochets. Some twenty feet in front of the chair stands a wall with five firing ports. The inmate may read a final statement before the warden places a hood over his or her head. The firing squad takes aim at the white cloth circle and fires simultaneously at the warden's command. The bullets rupture the heart, lungs, and major arteries, causing near instant death from shock and hemorrhage. The lower part of the chair in which the prisoner sits contains a pan to catch the flow of blood and other body fluids that rush out of the prisoner's body.

But the procedure doesn't always go as planned. Hal Schindler wrote about two instances where death by firing squad produced horrific results. The first was the execution of Wallace Wilkerson, sentenced to die for killing a man during an argument over a card game in Provo. He faced a firing squad in May 1879 without restraints. He had assured the local sheriff that he wanted to die like a man, looking the firing squad in the eye. As a result, the sheriff didn't blindfold or restrain Wilkerson.

It proved to be a terrible mistake. Just as the sheriff gave the command to take aim, Wilkerson shrugged his shoulders upward in anticipation of the impending bullets. Four bullets tore through his body. He jumped up, staggered several feet, and fell forward, crying out: "Oh, my God! My God! They've missed." Three of the four bullets entered Wilkerson's body above the heart. The fourth ripped into his arm. Witnesses reported that he lay writhing in pain for twenty-seven minutes before he was finally pronounced dead.

Hal Schindler also described a botched firing-squad execution in September 1951 at a new prison in Point of the Mountain, Utah. News reports at the time provided scant details of the execution. Twenty-five years later, *Tribune* reporter Clark Cobb unearthed information that only two of the four bullets fired from a distance of fifteen feet struck Eliseo Mares. They hit the inmate in the hip and abdomen, and it took several minutes for Mares to die — a much shorter period of time than with the more "humane" lethal injection preferred across the country today.

DEATH BY HANGING

If the firing squad is the most honorable method of execution, then hanging is the most ignominious. The hangman's rope, which measures from 0.75 to 1.25 inches in diameter and 30 feet in length, requires careful preparation before being used. Tied in accordance with military regulations, the hangman's knot must be treated with soap, wax, or oil so that the rope slips smoothly through the knot. To ensure that the rope will take the full force of the inmate's dropping body, the end of the rope is generally tied to a grommet in the ceiling and then to a metal T-bracket.

The restrained inmate is led to the gallows and ordered to stand over a trap door. Following an optional final statement, a hood is placed over the inmate's head and the hangman's knot is fixed around the neck behind the left ear to ensure that the neck snaps. All official hangings follow a military chart to determine the proper drop length based on the inmate's weight. The standard force applied to the neck from the drop is 1,260 pounds. If the rope is measured properly, the fall dislocates the third and fourth vertebrae, leading to a quick death. If it is not properly measured, the condemned may hang by the neck for minutes, slowly choking to death. In some cases, decapitation may occur.

According to the Espy File, approximately 13,350 people were executed by hanging in America between 1622 and 1987 — including 505 women. The youngest person ever hanged in the United States was a twelve-year-old Native American girl named Hannah Ocuish, executed in 1786 for the beating death of a six-year-old girl. The largest mass hanging in the country also involved Indians. On December 26, 1862, in Mankato, Minnesota, the U.S. government hanged thirty-eight Santee Sioux men because they left their reservation on a hunting expedition in search for food for their tribe. Minnesota governor Alexander Ramsey initially asked President Abraham Lincoln to order the execution of all 303 men in the hunting party.

Concerned about how Europe would view a mass hanging, Lincoln reached a compromise with Ramsey and other Minnesota politicians. He told them to pare the list to thirty-nine and he would order their immediate executions. He also promised to remove all Native Americans from the state, to give the state politicians $2 million, and to allow them to seize the reservation land. The condemned men — except one who received a last-minute reprieve — were hanged simultaneously, singing a Sioux death song.

The following day, Brigadier General H. H. Sibley sent President Lincoln the following message: "I have the honor to inform you that the 38 Indians and half-breeds ordered by you for execution were hung yesterday at Mankato at 10 A.M. Everything went off quietly, and the other prisoners are well-secured."

Lincoln also served as the cause of a far more celebrated mass hanging. Following his assassination by John Wilkes Booth on April 14, 1865, four of Booth's alleged coconspirators — George Atzerodt, David Herold, Lewis Powell (a.k.a. Paine), and Mary Elizabeth Surratt — were convicted and sentenced to hang. Their executions took place on July 7, 1865, in the yard of the Washington Arsenal prison. Captain Christian Rath drew a white canvas hood over each prisoner's neck and placed a noose over each of their heads. Assistants bound their arms and hands with cloth straps. Assistants also bound Mary Surratt's legs so that the kicking of her death struggle wouldn't immodestly reveal her undergarments. Rath ordered his helpers on the gallows platform to stand away from the traps. He clapped his hands three times, and on the third clap soldiers sprung the trap doors. The four prisoners fell.

"They bounded up again like a ball attached to a rubber band before they settled down," Rath commented after the hanging. It took twenty-five minutes for army surgeons to declare them all dead. Surratt holds the dubious distinction of being the first woman executed under federal law, even though many at the time — and many more today — believed she was innocent.

Public executions in America ended in 1936 after a mob of 20,000 people in Owensboro, Kentucky, showed up to watch the hanging of Rainey Bethea, a black man convicted of the rape and murder of a seventy-year-old white woman. But hanging behind prison walls continued in some states.

On May 27, 1994, Washington State hanged Charles Rodman Campbell, the next to last inmate to be hanged in the twentieth century.

Campbell was sentenced to die for murdering three women. At six foot two and weighing 224 pounds, he was unable to stand over the trap door, so authorities strapped his legs to a board. The drop fractured his C2 vertebra, but Campbell continued to have a heartbeat a full six minutes after the drop.

The last person hanged in the United States, Billy Bailey, died on January 25, 1996, executed by Delaware for the brutal murder of an elderly couple. His hanging was uneventful.

But some state hangings haven't fared as well. Tom "Black Jack" Ketchum, an obese killer, was decapitated when he dropped through the trap door in New Mexico on April 26, 1901. The same fate met the first woman executed in Arizona, fifty-two-year-old Eva Dugan, who had been convicted of the murder of her lover and employer. Her head jerked from her body on February 20, 1930, in front of seventy witnesses, including the first five women to witness an execution.

Not all the botched executions by hanging resulted in decapitation. Sometimes an improperly adjusted rope or miscalculated drop led to death by strangulation. San Quentin warden Clinton Duffy witnessed many of the 307 hangings carried out by California between 1893 and 1942, including the execution of Major Raymond Lisemba on May 9, 1942.

"The man hit bottom," Duffy said after the execution, "and I observed that he was fighting by pulling on the straps, wheezing, whistling, trying to get air, that blood was oozing through the black cap. I observed also that he urinated, defecated, and droppings fell on the floor, and the stench was terrible. I also saw witnesses pass out and have to be carried from the witness room. Some of them threw up."

Duffy added that it took ten minutes for Lisemba to die, and when his body was lowered and the black cap removed, the warden saw that the dead man's face had turned purple and his eyes had "popped" and "big hunks of flesh" had been torn off the side of his face where the noose had been.

DEATH BY GUILLOTINE

Deaths like these prompted some states to adopt what they deemed to be more humane methods of execution. In 1789, such reasoning prompted Joseph-Ignace Guillotin, a French doctor and member of the Revolutionary National Assembly, to invent the guillotine, a decapitating device that gained worldwide infamy during the French Revolution's Reign of Terror when thousands died in its grip.

Previous methods of execution in French society depended upon an individual's class. Swords lopped off the heads of nobles who could ensure a quick death by tipping the executioner. Commoners didn't enjoy this luxury. They often suffered the torture of drawing and quartering, a method of execution for treason that involved partial hanging or strangulation, disembowelment, then quartering — being cut into four pieces — before the ghastly ritual culminated in decapitation. (Monarchs often made examples of rebels by displaying these severed heads prominently in civic locations.)

In contrast, every man or woman who died by the guillotine died the same way. It was an egalitarian method of execution viewed as a social advance by a society caught up in the throes of creating a republic of virtue.

Charles-Louis Sanson, the official executioner of the French Revolution, said on April 25, 1792,

> Today the machine invented for the purpose of decapitating criminals sentenced to death will be put to work for the first time. Relative to the methods of execution practiced heretofore, this machine has

several advantages. It is less repugnant: no man's hands will be tainted with the blood of his fellow being, and the worst of the ordeal for the condemned man will be his own fear of death, a fear more painful to him than the stroke which deprives him of life.

By the time Maximilien Robespierre and his followers finished with the guillotine in their effort to eliminate those who failed to live up to the virtues expected from the republic of virtue, it had become one of the more feared instruments of state-sanctioned terror in the history of mankind. It produced the horrible spectacle of partially severed heads — requiring additional falls of the blade — and severed heads tumbling to the ground while blood gushed from bodies as hearts continued to pump. History suggests that the severed head retained consciousness for several terrible moments after it hit the ground, indicating that this death was not as quick as initially believed.

Perhaps that's why Hitler found the guillotine so appealing. He considered it a demeaning way to die, so he used it to carry out many of his political executions. His regime decapitated 20,000 people between 1942 and 1943 alone — more than the entire French Revolution.

DEATH BY GAS CHAMBER

It would be hard to devise a more expensive, dangerous, or cruel method of execution than death by gas chamber, which was designed and invented by Army Medical Corps officer Major Delos Turner and stands as the only execution device that requires the condemned to participate in his or her own execution, by inhaling lethal gas.

Dr. Allen McLean Hamilton, a toxicologist, first proposed the gassing of inmates to the state of Nevada, whose legislature adopted it as the state's official method of execution in 1921, replacing the electric chair.

Between 1930 and 1999, 955 men and 7 women died in gas chambers in eleven states: Arizona, California, Colorado, Maryland, Missouri, Mississippi, Nevada, New Mexico, North Carolina, Oregon, and Wyoming. Nevada came first with the gassing to death of Gee Jong on February 8, 1924, and Arizona last with a German national named Walter LeGrand on March 3, 1999. Four states, including Arizona, have retained the gas chamber as an alternative method of execution, even though it has proved to be anything but humane.

Death in a gas chamber usually takes six to eighteen minutes. It took eleven minutes before Donald Harding was pronounced dead in the Arizona gas chamber on April 6, 1992. The warden presiding over that execution said he would quit his job before carrying out another gas chamber execution.

The ritual of this form of execution begins when the condemned inmate is led into the death chamber and strapped into a chair by the arms, waist, ankles, and chest. A mask covers the inmate's face. The chamber is sealed. An executioner pours sulfuric acid down a tube into a metal container on the floor below a metal canister that contains cyanide pellets.

An open curtain allows witnesses to see the inmate in the chamber. If the inmate has a final statement, it is read. Then the warden signals the executioner, who hits an electric switch that opens the bottom of the metal canister and releases the cyanide pellets into the acid, unleashing a cloud of lethal gas.

Executions in a gas chamber are particularly hard to witness. The inmate's vomiting and convulsions indicate that his or her suffering is intense. Authorities encourage the inmate to inhale the gas deeply to bring on unconsciousness. He is told that if he attempts to hold his breath, wild convulsions will rack his body. A heart monitor alerts the warden in an adjacent control room to the inmate's death. It takes about half an hour to neutralize the poisonous gas in the death chamber before the inmate's body can be removed.

The electric chair can set inmates on fire and boil their brains. Flames shot out of John Louis Evans's head when he was electrocuted in Alabama in 1983. His gruesome demise is described in detail in the ensuing chapter "Death Row Redux." Lethal injection is discussed in "The Cocktail," which involves a three-drug potion used to kill inmates but which has been banned by veterinarians because there is no assurance that it does not cause excruciating pain.

The need for revenge that is wired so tightly into our psyches has produced scores of draconian methods for carrying out government approved executions. The guillotine and gas chamber are among the worst.

These and other methods of executing inmates and lingering questions about executing the innocent, should prompt the honest man to search his soul and seriously consider asking the state to ban the death penalty.

Human beings are more than the sum of their parts. We are not bound by survival behavior and the pleasure centers of our brains into an unholy alliance with sadism. We know that capital punishment is a crime.

2

Death Row Redux

Will the death penalty survive in the United States, or will the U.S. Supreme Court eventually strike it down, consigning it to history like drawing and quartering, burning at the stake, drowning, or boiling in oil? At first blush, the notion seems unlikely.

Death alone seems to satisfy the public's thirst for revenge for certain crimes. Prosecutors, victims, and the public call it justice. Criminals whom American juries have chosen to condemn must die to satisfy Everyman's notion of equity: an eye for an eye and a tooth for a tooth —an ancient cry for justice codified in 1760 B.C. by Hammurabi, the king of Babylon.

In their harsh quest for justice, Americans have frequently taken matters into their own hands to settle scores either real or imagined. Between 1882 and 1951 an estimated 4,730 lynchings took place in the United States, a period of vigilante justice when citizens either didn't wait for courts to act or disagreed with judicial verdicts or executive clemency.

Between 1608 and June 2, 1967 (the date of the last execution before the *Furman* moratorium), there were 14,489 executions in the United States sanctioned by law for crimes like trespassing, housebreaking, adultery, sodomy, piracy, slave revolts, and, of course, rape and murder. Between January 17, 1977 (the date of Gary Gilmore's execution in Utah, which ended the post-*Furman* moratorium on executions), and November 30, 2008, an additional 1,135 death sentences were carried out. Of those executed between 1608 and 1967, 49 percent were black. Of those executed since 1977, 34 percent were black. Of the 3,334 people executed in this country between 1930 and 1967 for the crime of murder, 2,066 were black. Of the 435 executed for rape, 405 were black.

Most of those executed for their crimes were men. Only thirty-two women died in American death chambers between 1930 and 1967. Since then, eleven more women have been executed. Of the inmates executed since 1977, twenty-two committed their crimes when they were under the age of eighteen. Hidden in all these statistics lies the undeniable fact that a disproportionate number of those either lynched or executed in America were poor, uneducated, or otherwise disadvantaged.

The infamous case of Leopold and Loeb shows that money and influence can ward off the death penalty. The two wealthy white teenage thrill-killers received life in prison for the brutal murder of a fourteen-year-old neighbor in Chicago in 1924. They had hired famed attorney Clarence Darrow to defend them.

Today, nationwide support for the death penalty

appears to be waning. In 2007 the Pew Research Center reported a 14 percent decline in support for capital punishment since 1996, when it enjoyed a 78 percent approval rating. If public support for the death sentence continues to erode, death penalty laws will change despite the hallowed concept of precedent. That, according to the eminent legal scholar Lawrence Friedman, is precisely how the American legal system works, the doctrine of *stare decisis* notwithstanding.

"Despite a strong dash of history and idiosyncrasy," Friedman wrote in *A History of American Law*, "the strongest ingredient in American law at any given time is the present: current emotions, real economic interests, concrete political groups."

If American approval of the death penalty is truly declining, as recent public opinion polls suggest, more states will follow the 2007 lead of New Jersey and abolish it. Will the death penalty be abolished nationally, its use restricted, or its method of death refined? No one can say. The American appetite for retribution rumbles constantly in the country's gut.

Beyond the emotional pleas articulated by death penalty abolitionists, there is an increasingly practical reason for ending the death penalty in America — a need to respect the government itself, which also appears to be at an all-time low. Various public opinion polls in 2008 revealed a dramatic decrease — as high as 82 percent disapproval rating — in the electorate's faith in its government.

American history provides a lesson in that regard. In the essays collected in The Federalist Papers, as Alexander Hamilton argued for ratifying the American Constitution — not a foregone conclusion in 1788 — he warned that American law would be too harsh unless the president had the power to pardon criminals.

"Humanity and good policy conspire to dictate that the benign prerogative of pardoning should be as little as possible fettered or embarrassed," he reasoned. "The criminal code of every country partakes so much of necessary severity that without an easy access to exceptions in favor of unfortunate guilt, justice would wear a countenance too sanguinary and cruel."

Hamilton's argument reflected a constitutional need for reason and mercy. New Jersey's decision to abolish the death penalty, the U.S. Supreme Court's 2007 decision to review lethal injection as cruel and unusual punishment, Nebraska's 2008 State Supreme Court ban on electrocutions, and the United Nations' 2007 resolution to eradicate the death penalty worldwide all indicate that the death penalty itself — not the mode of execution — is perhaps "too sanguinary and cruel."

Just thirty-five years ago, no one could have predicted a decline in U.S. support for the death penalty. After the Supreme Court struck down all capital punishment laws in the country in *Furman v. Georgia* in 1972, vacating the death sentences of 408 inmates, thirty-seven states and the federal government rushed to reenact death penalty statutes that would pass constitutional muster. The Supreme Court had ruled that the death penalty violated the Eighth Amendment's prohibition against cruel and unusual punishment because it wasn't applied evenly. The court did not say the death penalty was, per se, unconstitutional. The court's 5–4 decision in *Furman* set the stage for a new era of executions and a new method of death, one deemed more humane.

Utah became the first state to use its newly court-sanctioned death statute. In 1977 it executed Gary Gilmore, who insisted, to the chagrin of death penalty opponents, on being executed by firing squad. Between Gilmore's execution in 1977 through November 30, 2008, the states and the federal government executed 964 inmates by lethal injection, 155 by electrocution, 11 in the gas chamber, 3 by hanging, and 2 by firing squad.

At least forty of these executions went horribly wrong. Perhaps the most sensational was that of John Spenkelink, executed in Florida's electric chair on May 25, 1979, the second person to die following the *Furman* decision. Before he was dragged to the death chamber, he had reportedly been beaten, gagged, and had his neck broken by prison guards after he resisted their attempt to stuff cotton up his rectum — a common practice to prevent an inmate's bowel movement from catching on fire if it was released into the chair during execution. Some media reports held that Spenkelink had already died before guards strapped him into the electric chair.

Reports of abuse during his execution were so persistent that Florida authorities exhumed his body and performed an autopsy. Those same reports led the state to implement a policy of performing autopsies after each execution.

Such brutal abuse wasn't unfamiliar to Spenkelink. In February 1973, he shot Joseph Szymankiewicz twice and beat him in the head with a hatchet in Tallahassee, Florida. The men were traveling companions. The twenty-three-year-old Spenkelink said that the older, aggressive Szymankiewicz had raped him at gunpoint. Spenkelink said that when he managed to get the gun away from Szymankiewicz, he shot his forty-five-year-old rapist.

Spenkelink had an opportunity to plead guilty to a reduced charge of second-degree murder, which he refused. Taking a chance with the jury, he argued that he had killed Szymankiewicz in self-defense, but the jury found him guilty of first-degree murder and, absent mitigating evidence, sentenced him to death. Spenkelink thus became the first defendant convicted under the new death penalty statute that Florida enacted after the 1972 *Furman* ruling.

By August 1977, eighty-four men sat on Florida's death row with Spenkelink. He captured national media attention that September when Governor Reubin Askew signed his death warrant. His execution was scheduled for 8:30 A.M. on September 18, 1977. Death penalty opponents rallied around his case in an all-out attempt to prevent another post-*Furman* execution. These well-intentioned opponents succeeded in convincing a federal court to stay the death date, while death penalty advocates used his case to test the public's will to completely end the national moratorium on capital punishment that had been in place since June 2, 1967, when Louis Monge was put to death in Colorado's gas chamber. As the national debate on the death penalty intensified in the late 1960s, the states voluntarily decided to await a definitive ruling by the U.S. Supreme Court on this controversial issue before carrying out any more executions. That ruling came in *Furman v. Georgia*.

Because Gary Gilmore had asked to be put to death, his execution had not really put an end to the *Furman*-related moratorium. It was Spenkelink's case that drew the death penalty battle lines in the proverbial sand on the moratorium issue. Both sides of the issue advanced old and new arguments in every public media venue. Through it all, Spenkelink remained calm, a silent man caught up in the noisy demands to kill or spare him. Perhaps his silence masked his fear or expressed his courage. The only thing that mattered to him was time — and that precious commodity was slowly ebbing away.

By early 1978, Spenkelink's situation had become tenuous, and he knew it. Press accounts about his case referred to the "final appeal" he had pending before the Supreme Court. In February the nation's highest court rejected it. His case quickly went to Florida's Executive Clemency Board, which consisted of the governor and his cabinet.

Spenkelink remained quiet and steady in his death cell, an enclosed world of concrete and steel painted a dull green — a toilet without a seat, a small face bowl, and a steel bunk. He woke daily at 6:30 A.M. for a breakfast that generally consisted of powdered eggs, dry cereal, and undrinkable coffee. At 11:30 A.M. he ate lunch and at 4:00 P.M. dinner, each usually consisting of potatoes, rice, bread, hamburger, canned ham, or beef stew. The state had supplied a 15-inch black-and-white television set. He was allowed to go to a recreation yard twice a week for two hours of exercise. Every other day he was allowed a five-minute shower. He was allowed visitors on Saturdays and Sundays between 9:00 A.M. and 3:00 P.M. On Fridays and Mondays, he received an aluminum razor for shaving. He could spend up to $15 a week in the prison canteen on cigarettes, sodas, and other drugstore goods. The Florida Division of Corrections Industries issued him ten packs of non-filtered cigarettes each week. During the summer, his cell boiled because there were no fans, and during the winter it froze because it lacked sufficient heat.

Spenkelink was living in a cage engulfed in constant noise: television sets, radios, cell doors slamming, the screams of nightmares, and conversations shouted between cells. There is no living hell comparable to the compressed, haunted world of death row.

Finally, on Friday, May 18, 1979, Governor Bob Graham signed the death warrants for Spenkelink, white, and Willie Jasper Darden Jr., black. Spenkelink's execution date was set for Wednesday, May 23, at 7:00 A.M. and Darden's for 8:00 A.M. that same day. Darden was used as a red herring. His case had never been to federal court, so a stay of execution was inevitable. Governor Graham's legal counsel surely apprised the governor of that fact, and since the governor signed Darden's death warrant anyway, we can reasonably assume that he wanted to force death penalty opponents to wage their fight on two fronts.

Darden's death warrant absolved Florida of the usual charge of racism leveled in any death penalty debate in a Deep South state. It showed that the state was willing to execute a white man and a black man at the same time. As expected, Darden received a stay of execution from a federal judge on May 22.

On May 21 and May 22, the Florida attorney general's office had three planes in the air flying around the country to prevent any last-minute stays of execution in the case. There have been few, if any, examples in death penalty history where a state worked so methodically to see a sentence carried out. The entire legal machinery of Florida focused on one objective: the execution of John Spenkelink.

Still, Spenkelink said nothing. He made out a twenty-nine-word will to his sister that read: "This is to authorize the release of my body and all my personal belongings immediately if I'm executed (murdered) by the State of Florida to Mrs. Carol Dean Meyers."

Despite the efforts of the Florida attorney general to prevent it, a stay of execution was issued anyway. As the final hour approached, it was granted by U.S. Supreme Court Justice Thurgood Marshall, shortly after Justice Lewis Powell refused to issue a stay. On hearing news of the Marshall stay, Spenkelink reportedly said, "Thank God." Fifth Circuit Court of Appeals judge Elbert Tuttle of Atlanta also weighed in on the issue by granting his own stay of execution.

The relief, however, proved short-lived. The Florida attorney general's office worked feverishly all day Wednesday to lift the stays. On Thursday morning, other justices of the U.S. Supreme Court overturned Marshall's stay, and later that same night, at 9:30 P.M., a three-judge panel of the Fifth Circuit overturned Tuttle's. The message had been sent clearly through the judicial pipeline. No other judge dared issue another stay.

Spenkelink remained in a holding cell next to the death chamber as the last-minute legal maneuverings came to an end. His head, wrists, and ankles had been shaved in preparation for his appointment with the electric chair. Realizing the end was drawing near, Spenkelink gave a final statement to Reverend Tom Teamster, which read: "Man is what he chooses to be. He chooses that for himself." Spenkelink then took Holy Communion. At 9:50 A.M. on Friday morning, the final legal door slammed shut when the U.S. Supreme Court refused one last request for a stay.

It is unclear at what point prison guards allegedly tried to stuff cotton up his rectum, but it probably came right before or shortly after the Supreme Court rejected that final stay request. Spenkelink resisted this final indignity. The guards did what they naturally do when confronted with inmate resistance: they used physical force.

At 10:00 A.M., Spenkelink was strapped into Florida's electric chair. Thirty-two witnesses had assembled to observe the execution. Prison Superintendent David Brierton stalled the execution until Governor Graham gave him the final order to proceed at 10:11 A.M.

"There are no stays at this time," Graham said. "May God be with us."

Spenkelink could not speak as he sat in the chair. Prison guards had gagged him. They didn't want him speaking about the beating he had just endured.

"He looked terrified," said Tom Slaughter, an Associated Press reporter who witnessed the execution.

Brierton placed a black hood over Spenkelink's head at 10:12 A.M. and signaled for the first of three 2,300-volt electrical charges to be sent through the prisoner's head. Smoke filled the death chamber. Spenkelink's flesh sizzled until it turned black. He was pronounced dead at 10:18 A.M. on May 25, 1979.

Death penalty proponents achieved a significant victory with Spenkelink's execution. His death signaled that the national death penalty moratorium had officially ended. States had a new license to kill, sanctioned by the Supreme Court.

Why the rush to resume executions?

The American public felt as battered by violent crime in the late twentieth century as it did during the two hundred years between 1608 and 1808 when it executed nearly 150 slaves for doing what was natural under the bondage of slavery: revolting against their masters.

The death penalty is a violent response to violence. The 72,000 executions in sixteenth century England during the long reign of Henry VIII by boiling, burning at the stake, hanging, beheading, and drawing and quartering for any of the 222 crimes punishable by death offer irrefutable evidence of the violent, criminal roots of the death penalty in English common law. A state-sanctioned death penalty, rooted in ancient codes of revenge and retaliation, is more methodical and violent in its cold and unfeeling brutality than most crimes.

On April 22, 1983, Alabama proved that once again when it executed John Louis Evans III, who, along with codefendant Wayne Ritter, killed a man in an armed robbery during an interstate crime spree. Corrections officials botched the Evans execution, literally frying him with repeated jolts of electricity. It took three surges of 1,900 volts and ten terror-filled minutes to kill him.

Reports were still circulating about Spenkelink's broken neck when the Alabama debacle occurred. While we may never know what really happened to Spenkelink, it is clear what happened to Evans: he was quite literally roasted to death. His execution was an inexcusable travesty. How else to explain the belated clemency plea by Corrections Commissioner Fred Smith and Warden J. B. White to Governor George Wallace at the request of Evans's lawyer following the second jolt of electricity that sent flames bursting out of Evans's left temple? It would have been more humane had prison guards simply rolled a grenade into the death chamber.

Smith ordered a halt to the execution after the third charge of electricity as he awaited a reply from Wallace's office on the clemency request. Evans was pronounced dead. The governor had the presence of mind not to intervene. He danced "with those who brung him," as the old southern saying on loyalty goes.

Obnoxious letters to the editors of local newspapers followed, demonstrating once again the South's rabid love of biblical justice. Virtually all of the letters praised the execution. One called for the impeachment of a federal judge who gave Evans an eleventh-hour stay.

"Hell, I don't feel sorry for him — he got what he deserved" was the sentiment of some of these Bible-toting zealots, the same ones no doubt seen on local streets opposing abortion.

Christianity has no brief for sadistic pleasure in the death of another. The prime lesson of the New Testament is forgiveness. But humans have a deep-seated thirst for the blood of those they deem transgressors. It is particularly common to those who live in the South. It is virtually worshiped in Harris County, Texas, the death penalty capital of the Western world.

An execution should be a solemn affair. The government is taking the ultimate action against an individual, extinguishing his or her right to life. When the state exercises this awesome power, it should have the moral decency to do it as quickly and painlessly as possible. It is not an occasion that invites gloating and celebration from its citizenry — not even from the victims of the crimes.

If any decency emanated from the travesty of

Evans's execution, it was the way the condemned man conducted himself in the final moments of his life. He did not cry, fawn, or beg. His body simply arched forward in silent agony, without protest, while prison officials let the situation ratchet out of control. A prison chaplain violated his request that his final words be kept confidential, blurting out those final words: "I have no malice for anyone, no hatred for anyone."

Less than five months after Evans's execution, the Supreme Court refused to block the execution of Jimmy Lee Gray, a convicted child rapist and murderer, who had spent seven years on death row trying to avoid Mississippi's gas chamber. As a matter of decency, Reverend Henry Hudson visited Gray in his death cell at the Parchman prison and delivered the news about the Supreme Court ruling.

Often described as a computer whiz and a born-again Christian, Gray accepted the news calmly. Although he wanted to live, he had grown tired of fighting his death sentence. The lonely struggle of trying to escape the inevitable had drained him of hope.

Gray spent his last day on earth meeting with friends and ministers, including Hollis Allred, a Natchez church leader who worked with inmates, and Reverend Don Dickerson, who had driven from Hurst, Texas, to be with him before the execution. Gray spoke by telephone with members of his immediate family — his mother, father, and brothers, all of whom lived out of state. His mother had twice asked state officials to execute her son. No one in the family would either attend the execution or claim Gray's body. Allred's church had made plans give him a Christian burial.

The last-minute death ritual was not new to Gray.

He had been close to execution several times before, only to be spared by a last-minute stay. But this time was different. Bill Allain, Mississippi's attorney general, was about to be elected governor on a law-and-order plank that had called for Gray's execution. Mississippi had not used its lethal, six-sided execution chamber since 1964. Anticipating Gray's execution, prison officials tested the stainless steel chamber, killing a small animal in one of those tests.

When the Supreme Court refused to halt Gray's execution, Mississippi corrections commissioner Morris Thigpen told reporters gathered at the prison that it was "more than likely" the execution would take place. Gray's lawyer, Dennis Balske of Montgomery, Alabama, said there would be no further appeals. "We have reached the final word and we take it as final," he said. Before leaving his office to attend the execution, Balske told reporters that the Supreme Court decision had shut off all legal avenues and "we really have nowhere else to go."

Just as bread is made of flour, the death penalty is made of revenge. A tremendous hunger in society clamored for revenge in Gray's case. While Gray was preparing to die, the father of the girl he had killed, Richard Scales, who lived in Dallas, told reporters, "I will be waiting at home for word of the execution. I want to know when it happens, because it will be a relief."

Not everyone felt that way. A dozen death penalty opponents arrived at the prison, which was on the highest security alert. But Thigpen said the prison was "surprisingly quiet and very orderly."

"Killing does not show other people that killing is wrong," David Flockhart, a regional coordinator for Amnesty International, told the small group of protestors.

Outgoing governor William Winter had made it clear that he would not intervene in the execution, but he kept the telephone line to the death chamber open in the event of another last-minute stay. Another group of fifty to sixty protestors had gathered in front of his antebellum mansion for a candlelight vigil.

The last few minutes of Gray's life took place in the "last-night room" adjacent to the execution chamber. At 12:14 A.M. on September 2, 1983, Jackson County sheriff John Ledbetter led Gray, clad in a red death-row jumpsuit, from this cell. Thigpen reported that Gray was calm, seemingly having accepted his fate. He was strapped into a black metal chair in the middle of the execution chamber. At Thigpen's direction, cyanide tablets dropped into a bowl of acid below the chair, unleashing white wisps of lethal cyanide gas.

Gray inhaled deeply three times to hasten his death. His body jerked violently against the straps binding his arms, chest, and legs. For the next eight minutes, Gray's head slumped forward, then abruptly flung back. It was reported that the thirty-four-year-old self-styled poet moaned fourteen times before falling silent. Listening through a remote stethoscope attached to Gray's chest, doctors pronounced him dead within two minutes, despite prolonged bodily spasms.

Balske strongly disagreed with the official claim that Gray had met a "quick end." He said his client suffered a "painful death." At one point, Gray's head struck a metal pole attached to the back of the chair so hard it shook the entire death chamber.

"Hell, he was in pain," Balske said.

A hearse took Gray's body to a funeral home in Indianola, about forty miles from the prison. Following an unannounced 7:00 A.M. service, Gray was laid to rest in an undisclosed plot. The funeral home director told reporters that he had been buried in Sunflower County, where the Parchman prison farm is located.

"Even in prison he had been able to talk, to breathe and to laugh, and he had taken all these things from my little girl," Scales said, continuing to stoke the flames of revenge. "He didn't have the right to continue to live."

Following the botched executions of Spenkelink, Evans, and Gray by traditional American methods — the gas chamber and the electric chair — most death penalty states decided to follow the 1977 lead of Oklahoma, which had adopted lethal injection as its official method of execution. They wanted to escape the image of Thomas Wolfe's Old South and usher in the New South with a kinder, gentler way of killing people. Today, thirty-five states and the federal government use this "more humane" method to execute condemned inmates. Seven states offer options to the condemned: gas chamber, hanging, or firing squad.

The first lethal injection was carried out in 1982 when Texas put Charles Brooks to death. But this method of killing inmates has not proved to be any more humane than the electric chair or gas chamber. Much like the guillotine in France, adopted in the eighteenth century as a more benign form of execution than boiling or burning at the stake, lethal injection hasn't lived up to its hype. It, too, has produced horribly botched executions.

One of the most publicized cases involved another Florida inmate, Angel Diaz, who suffered a thirty-four-minute lethal injection ordeal in 2006 before he finally died. The state had to use two doses of the deadly cocktail of drugs before doctors could pronounce him dead.

A subsequent autopsy revealed that the needles had been pushed through the prisoner's veins directly into the muscle tissue of his arms.

Five months later, it took Ohio prison officials an hour and a half to execute Christopher Newton. The process took so long that prison officials allowed Newton to take a bathroom break during their struggle to locate a suitable vein in his arm for the needle. At one point, the condemned man became so frustrated with the process that he asked prison officials, "Can you just give me something by mouth to end this?"

In a *Los Angeles Times* column on November 26, 2007, Eric Berger, who teaches constitutional law at the University of Nebraska, wrote about the need for a more humane method of administering lethal injections: "Execution by lethal injection need not be so inherently painful. Experts agree that other drugs could cause death without the risk of also causing undue suffering. Because the states have selected drugs that are so sensitive to error, however, it is imperative that they employ the right people to administer them. But numerous states employ people who are manifestly unfit."

While *Furman v. Georgia* opened the door to a new era of executions, the mid-1990s produced a new federal law that accelerated the death march. In April 1996, President Bill Clinton signed the Antiterrorism and Effective Death Penalty Act, which severely limited access to the federal writ of habeas corpus by state prisoners, especially those with a death sentence. AEDPA, as it is known in the courts, was enacted with a specific intent to allow states to speed up the death penalty process. It has accomplished that objective: Of the 1,135 executions carried out in this country between 1977 through November 30, 2008, 30 percent occurred in the two decades prior to AEDPA, while a staggering 70 percent occurred after its enactment. AEDPA more than doubled the rate of execution in the United States.

Botched executions notwithstanding, the death penalty's sordid reign in America continues. The rush to judgment in cases that stoke revenge is not easily slowed. The baleful sounds and smells of state-sanctioned death will persist until the nation recognizes that capital punishment is barbarism cloaked in Old Testament vengeance.

3

Whim and Caprice

This nation's criminal justice system was founded on the noble ideals of fairness and equality, but subsequent history reveals little of them. Color, social status, gender, and religion largely determine the administration of justice in criminal cases. Discriminatory justice has always played out, and will continue, in courtrooms across the country. If you believe otherwise, you've never had a jailer's foot up your ass or a cop's club on the side of your head.

The most visible aspect of the discrimination that pervades the American justice system is its racism. The race of the offender and the victim — especially in the South — has always determined the quality of justice in this part of the country. In either the Old South or the New South, where blood, violence, and casual disregard for life adhere in the cultural mindset, the death penalty has always met with a support like religious fervor. Not long ago, blacks were routinely lynched in the South for committing crimes against white people from murder to "failing to comprehend their place." Thomas Wolfe captured the mindset of lynch justice in *The Web and the Rock*.

> They cry: "How are y', Jim? Is it hot enough fer you?'
>
> And Jim will say, with a brisk shake of the head: "Hotter'n what Sherman said war was, ain't it, Ed?"
>
> And the street will roar with hearty, red-faced laughter: "By God! That's a good 'un. Damned if ole Jim didn't have it about right too!" — but the eyes keep going back and forth, and fear, suspicion, hatred, and mistrust, and something stricken in the South long, long ago, is there among them.
>
> And after a day before the drug stores or around the empty fountain in the Courthouse Square, they go out to lynch a nigger. They kill him, and they kill him hard. They get in cars at night and put the nigger in between them, they go down the dusty roads until they find the place that they are going to, and before they get there, they jab little knives into the nigger, not a long way, not the whole way in, but just a little way. And they laugh to see him squirm. When they get out at the place where they are going to, the place the nigger sat in is a pool of blood. Perhaps it makes the boy who is driving the car sick at his stomach, but the older people laugh. Then they take the nigger through the rough field stubble of a piece of land and hang him to a tree. But before they hang him

they saw off his thick nose and his fat nigger lips with a rusty knife. And they laugh about it. Then they castrate him. And at the end they hang him.

Blacks in the South had to deal with this kind of lynch mob justice as late as the 1970s. The federal government eventually applied sufficient law enforcement and political pressure on southern states to put an end to the "unofficial" executions of blacks outside the justice system, but it did little to root out the lynch mob mindset. It continues to manifest itself in the way that juries in these states disproportionately sentence blacks to death. Two-thirds of the more than 3,000 executions carried out from 1930 through 1967, and 936 of the 1,135 executions carried out from 1977 through November 30, 2008, took place in the South. More than half of the inmates executed for murder in America between 1930 and 2007 were black, and for rape the figure was 90 percent.

So it was fitting that just past midnight on December 7, 1982, Charles Brooks, a black man, looked at his girlfriend through a window in the Texas death chamber at Huntsville, told her he loved her, and urged her to be strong. Then, as a fast-acting barbiturate surged through his veins, he yawned and died. Brooks was the first person executed in this nation by lethal injection. *Time* magazine called his death "the most significant execution in years." It was indeed — a clear manifestation of the southern lynch mentality.

Brooks and a codefendant named Woody Loudres had received death sentences for the kidnap-murder of a Fort Worth auto mechanic named David Gregory during a 1976 car theft/robbery. The two men bound Gregory's hands and feet before a single bullet pierced his brain.

An appeals court later reversed Loudres's conviction and sentence. The state elected not to retry him for capital murder. The prosecution offered, and Loudres accepted, a forty-year plea bargain — a sentence of which he served just eleven years.

Loudres's plea bargain rightly disturbed some — the South has its freethinkers — including Jack Strickland, the former Tarrant County district attorney who prosecuted both Brooks and Loudres. Along with former Texas attorney general Waggoner Carr, Strickland appeared before the Texas Board of Pardons and Paroles in an effort to prevent Brooks's execution.

"I'm in a difficult position in the sense that, when I prosecuted this man," Strickland said, "I thought it [the death sentence] was appropriate. To this day, the State of Texas does not know which defendant fired [the fatal shot]."

"One of them should not be killed and the other one given 40 years," Carr agreed, appearing before the clemency board on behalf of the Criminal Defense Lawyers Association.

But the clemency board turned a deaf ear, voting 2–1 against a stay of execution. Governor Bill Clements accepted the board's decision.

In prison Brooks had converted to Islam. He was a devoutly religious man. He was waging a fight to live without anger or bitterness. "Morally, I did not knowingly or intentionally cause anybody's death," Brooks said in a media interview, although he acknowledged being present when Gregory was killed. "I have had to carry this fact that this man no longer lives because of my involvement. I have regretted tremendously my participating in the events of that particular day."

Brooks refused to express any bitterness toward Loudres for escaping the death sentence. "He felt that people shouldn't be mad at Woody," Imam Akbar Nuriddin Shabazz, the prison's Muslim chaplain, told reporters.

The Fifth Circuit Court of Appeals rejected Brooks's final request for a stay of execution, saying: "Our granting of yet another stay at this late hour for further review of claims so often considered and of such little merit would be an abdication of our duty."

The judicial die had been cast. Charles Brooks was executed. *Time* magazine reported of the execution that "the apparent unfairness is plain and jarring, if not unconstitutional."

The Brooks execution was not only morally unfair, it underscored the legal whim and caprice of the application of the death penalty in those early years as the federal courts grappled with the states' desire to execute prisoners post-*Furman*. Or as Louisiana Supreme Court justice James Dennis said during oral arguments in a death penalty case: "Let's get it on the road. Let's get these death penalties moving."

Colin Clark and Michael Glover were convicted of the 1978 murder of Fred Schmidt, the manager of a Red Lobster restaurant in Baton Rouge. Like David Gregory, Schmidt was shot in the back of the head with a .38-caliber pistol — then stabbed thirty times with a butcher knife. Glover received a life sentence, while Clark was sentenced to death after Glover testified that Clark had killed Schmidt.

In the latter part of 1981, Clark fired his attorneys, dropped his appeal, and, like Gary Gilmore, informed an astonished public that he would rather die than spend the rest of his life in prison. The people of Louisiana and much of the rest of the country followed the media's every detail of Clark's effort to become the first post-*Furman* inmate put to death in Louisiana's refurbished electric chair.

The Fifth Circuit Court of Appeals granted his mother's appeal that he not be executed before a sanity hearing could be conducted — which cut short his voluntary journey to the death chamber. After a Baton Rouge federal district court declared him sane, Clark resumed his appeals, now claiming that Glover had actually killed Schmidt. The case went back to the Fifth Circuit.

On the morning of December 7, 1982, just after Charles Brooks had been put to death in Texas, Clark turned on his television set and learned that the Fifth Circuit had reversed his conviction on the same constitutional issue that, scant hours before, it had declared "of such little merit" in the Brooks case. The issue was the same in both cases: Which defendant killed the victim? Clark or Glover? Brooks or Loudres?

The Fifth Circuit said in reversing Colin Clark's conviction:

> While there was ample evidence of a conspiracy between Clark and Glover to commit a crime as the Louisiana Supreme Court held . . . , that crime was armed robbery and not murder. Even if it could be said that the evidence warranted a finding of conspiracy to kill (and we cannot say so), the jury was not required to find that a conspiracy to kill existed or told that absent that conspiracy they could not attribute the murderous act of one conspirator to the other. . . . [Clark] had the personal grievance; he had carried a knife which resembled the weapon found beside the body; his hand was badly cut at the

time. Before the Constitution will allow this conviction and sentence, however, we must know that
the jury found beyond any reasonable doubt that
Clark, personally, did have that mind to kill.

The Constitution didn't have any problem letting
Brooks die. Although Brooks had a stronger constitutional claim than Clark, he was black. A black man died,
while the court spared a white man who wanted to die.
Time magazine noted this irony two weeks after Brooks's
execution, saying it "surprised knowledgeable lawyers"
because "Brooks' grounds for appeal seemed as strong as
those in hundreds of other cases that are pending."

Why was Brooks's case rushed through the appellate process? What was the real difference between Clark
and Brooks? How could the Constitution spare one condemned inmate in Louisiana and kill another in Texas on
the same legal issue? Why did Texas, with 172 condemned inmates to choose from at the time, select a
black man to be its first post-*Furman* execution? Why
was Ronald O'Bryan, the infamous Candy Man killer —
a white man who murdered his own child for insurance
money — spared just months before Brooks was executed? Why did the U.S. Supreme Court select the case
of Thomas Andy Barefoot, a white killer in Texas, over
Brooks's case to decide the issue of how federal courts
should deal with emergency death penalty appeals?

As *Time* pointed out in a cover story on January 4,
1983, in the wake of the Brooks execution, "There is always caprice along the way to death row. Prosecutors
have great leeway in deciding which homicides to try as
capital murders. A killer can be persuaded to testify

against an accomplice to save his own life. Brooks was convicted and executed; for the same murder his partner must serve only eight more years in prison."

Official caprice and whim indeed run deep in the system.

"You can have all the correct issues for appeal," Scharlette Holdman, director of Florida's Clearinghouse on Criminal Justice, told *Time*, "but if you don't have a good lawyer to raise them, they don't mean a damn thing."

Beyond legal issues like "ineffective legal representation," ethnicity often becomes the deciding factor in the quality of judicial review in capital cases. Of the 1,135 post-*Furman* executions through November 30, 2008, 80 percent of the cases involved white victims, even though Justice Department statistics show that blacks, through 2006, were six times more likely to be victims of homicides than whites. And only 14 percent of those 1,135 execution cases involved black victims.

That racially skewed quality of judicial review came to the fore in the J. D. "Cowboy" Autry case. On April 20, 1980, a Texas convenience store clerk named Shirley Drouet told Autry, "That will be $2.70" for a six-pack of beer he had placed on the store's counter. Autry shot the clerk between the eyes with a .38-caliber pistol, saying: "Here's your $2.70."

Autry was scheduled to die in Texas on December 17, 1982, when Texas put Brooks to death. But just thirty-four hours before Autry was to be strapped to the same gurney on which Brooks had died, he received a reprieve. As it turned out, this cold-blooded killer had no idea that he stood less than a year away from a high legal drama that would make him famous, landing him a cover story in *Newsweek* and a permanent place in death penalty legal lore.

For the next ten months, Autry's case behaved like any of the other Texas death penalty cases moving up and down the appeals ladder. Just weeks after Mississippi carried out its first post-*Furman* execution, Port Arthur judge Leonard Giblin set October 5, 1983, as Autry's third execution date. Judge Giblin felt Autry was a perfect candidate for execution.

Appointed counsel made routine appeals of Autry's execution date and all were summarily denied. Then on October 3, the Supreme Court refused to stay the execution. At that point, ACLU attorneys joined the case, raising the legal issue of proportionality — a constitutional standard for reviewing death sentences to ensure they were imposed fairly.

On October 4, Autry was transferred to the prison's death holding cell at Huntsville. He had seventeen hours to live. Later that morning, a federal district judge heard his proportionality argument and denied the request for a stay. That afternoon, his attorneys gathered in a conference room in Marshall, Texas, and presented their legal arguments by telephone to three judges of the Fifth Circuit Court of Appeals, all located in different cities.

Meanwhile Autry spoke to family members by telephone. When one of them asked if the execution was going to be carried out, he replied, "I believe so. . . . It don't scare me no more. I'm ready for it. I've had time to prepare for it."

Five hours later, at 10:45 P.M., Autry heard a radio news bulletin that the Fifth Circuit had refused to block his execution. Fifteen minutes later, a prison chaplain and a dozen guards opened his cell door and escorted him to the 12-by-18 death chamber. Guards took up their standard antiresistance positions — but Autry didn't want to fight. He said he only wanted to die like a man. He jumped on the gurney to be strapped down. *Newsweek* reported:

> His courage lasted until the three-inch white straps had been buckled around his body, his wrists and his ankles and his hands had been taped down to the lateral supports. Then the terror engulfed him; he felt as if he were sinking in it, drowning in a black fear deeper than any he had ever known. It was 11:03 when they finished. He had 58 minutes left. At 11:05 he felt a sharp sting in one arm and then the other as the catheters were inserted just below the elbow. It was done by paramedics, since the canons of ethics forbade participation by doctors, and one made a bad job of it. J. D. looked down at his left arm. There was blood from the elbow to the wrist. He broke into a boiling sweat. *I'm gonna die*, he thought.
>
> He lay there mute, chewing gum to hide his terror, suspended in a purgatory of time. Above his head was the ceiling vent from the days of Old Sparky, built to draw off the stench of incontinence and burning flesh. The i.v. tubes snaked upward from his arms to a curtained window in the wall between him and unseen executioners; they were already flooded with saline solution, the medium for the lethal cocktail of three chemicals that would follow. From outside, he could hear a rising visceral tide of noise, inchoate at first, louder and clearer as his hour drew near. A crowd had formed, a few demonstrators praying by candlelight for his life, a

vastly larger number of high-school and college students howling for his death. One man was later arrested packing a gun; others waved signs that said WE PAY FOR OUR BEER and, over a picture of a beer can and a needle, THIS BUD'S FOR YOU. The time ticked toward midnight, and the sound outside congealed into an insistent rhythmic chant: "Kill him! Kill him! Kill him!"

While guards were strapping Autry to the gurney, ACLU attorney Alvin Bronstein, a legendary figure in the anti–death penalty movement, was sitting in a deserted alcove of the U.S. Supreme Court, where he learned that the Fifth Circuit had denied Autry's stay request. On a yellow legal pad, Bronstein wrote out by hand a three-page legal argument on the issue of proportionality. Court clerks delivered the handwritten petition, put together without much hope of success, to Associate Justice Byron White. Just sixteen minutes before midnight, and just thirty-one minutes before Autry was to be put to death, Justice White issued a stay of execution. The stay gave the high court an opportunity to rule on the proportionality issue, but the last-minute intervention triggered howls of protest from Texas officials.

"I was very sorry to see these matters have to be resolved at the last moment," said Governor Mark White. "It seems regrettable we cannot handle judicial appeals without waiting to the last 20 minutes before an execution is to be carried out. It seems ridiculous that all the lawyers that have been brought to bear on this case and all the judges couldn't have done a better job."

"The effect of the stay order is to stay most proceedings in all Texas death penalty cases," said Texas attorney general Jim Mattox, who was quick to point out that the proportionality issue had been rejected in the Brooks case.

"Now, members of the Supreme Court seem to be telling us a different story . . . in Justice White's stay," Mattox lamented. "Justice delayed is justice denied. It brings about a healthy disrespect for our judicial system."

A family member of one of Autry's victims joined in the crescendo of criticism. "One day they say let him die," the relative said. "Why change your mind the next day? No make sense."

Newsweek, trying to find a balance in the controversy, observed that

> a sort of justice had been done, however one felt about the larger issue of capital punishment or the bloody particularities of the life and crimes of J. D. Autry. The processes of the law had worked swiftly and efficiently through most of his three-year passage under judgment, and if the end game had a ragged and hasty look, it was because the system had worked — because a single justice had decided in the night that a last measure of fairness was more important than haste in a capital case.

A good point. One month earlier, on the afternoon of the day Mississippi executed its first post-*Furman* inmate, Jimmy Lee Gray, his lawyer had told the news media "we really have nowhere to go." The Supreme Court had just rejected a stay of execution. There was no late-afternoon telephone conference with Fifth Circuit judges or a lawyer sitting in the alcove of the high court preparing a last-minute handwritten appeal. Yet the proportionality issue was every bit as applicable in Gray's case as it was in Autry's case.

But in the end, the proportionality issue did not save J. D. Autry. He was put to death on March 14, 1984, declining to make a last statement. His false bravado failed him in the end.

Both prosecutorial and judicial whim and caprice have always played pivotal roles in death penalty cases. A black person can kill an entire black family, and a white district attorney will let him plead out to reduced charges. But another black person can kill one white victim, and the same white district attorney will demand the death penalty. That sort of whim is why Charles Brooks was executed and Colin Clark was not. They both were convicted of killing a white man, execution-style, during the commission of a crime. The only difference? Brooks was black, and Clark was white.

That the proportionality argument was held to apply in the Autry case and not the Brooks case underscores the whimsical and capricious nature of the judicial system. These whims and caprices have created a legacy of injustice in too many of the 1,135 post-*Furman* execution cases.

The attitude behind them stems from the South's love of lynching, which was reflected yet again in the crowd of approximately three hundred white students, mostly from law enforcement classes, who braved that cold predawn morning in December 1982 to stand in front of the Huntsville prison and celebrate Brooks's execution, proudly waving placards that read: "Justice Finally Prevails" and "Kill 'em in the Vein—Make it Good."

4

Surviving

I spent five years, eight months, and twenty-two days on death row at the Louisiana State Penitentiary. I was number C-43 — the forty-third person placed on death row since its opening in 1956 after the state shifted executions from the parish jails to Angola. I was also one of the 408 condemned inmates across the country spared execution by *Furman v. Georgia*.

Sitting at my desk in a high-rise condo in downtown Houston in 2007, searching the Internet for information about botched executions for an article I was preparing for the John T. Floyd Law Firm's Web site, I came across *The Execution Tapes*, an hour-long PBS special hosted by Ray Suarez that featured excerpts from audio tapes of twenty-two Georgia executions.

As I listened to the recording of the 1984 execution of a convicted murderer named Ivon Ray Stanley, a flood of memories rushed into my mind. Although I had written extensively about the death penalty and its sordid history, the banality and indifference exhibited by officials during Stanley's execution shocked me. It was soul-wrenching. You do not hear Stanley's voice on the tapes — they are a play-by-play description of his death delivered in the voice of a rural Georgia assistant prison warden. But it doesn't take much imagination to visualize Stanley's death as it unfolds in the warden's narrative.

At the end of the execution, the corrections officials — to whom the assistant warden had been speaking while recording the execution — praised him for the "great job" he had done in carrying out the execution. Those officials obviously didn't want Georgia to attract the bad press endured by Alabama and Mississippi following the botched 1983 executions of John Evans and Jimmy Lee Gray. Pleased by the praise, the assistant warden responded to his superiors in his Georgia accent: "Send us another one on down here."

I sat back in my chair, trying to comprehend the enormity of the recording. These were rural, twangy-voiced, hard-bitten southern prison officials whose attitudes about humanity and punishment derived from a race-obsessed culture that has always found pleasure in the suffering of others. With 990 executions (through November 30, 2008) to its credit since 1608, Georgia ranks fourth in putting people to death in the United States.

I know this kind of rural southern prison official well, having spent so many years in the Louisiana prison system with their boots on my neck. Although I was spared Ivon Ray Stanley's brutal fate, many times during my forty years in prison I felt the death penalty would have been more merciful than the life sentence I ultimately received after my death sentence was overturned. These were moments of depression born of utter hopelessness when the human soul is beaten down and stomped into a corner.

In March 2007, the Gulf Region Advocacy Center (GRACE) asked me to speak with an inmate housed in Houston's county jail named Robert Mason, who had served sixteen years on a robbery conviction before cold case detectives linked him to an earlier contract murder. Detectives visited Mason at the Texas prison where he was serving the robbery sentence to question him about the murder. Initially he denied involvement, but then he gave them a full confession.

Armed with that confession and other corroborating evidence, the Harris County District Attorney's Office stated its intention to seek the death penalty against Mason. His court-appointed attorneys persuaded the district attorney's office to accept a plea bargain for a lesser sentence of life imprisonment — one that would require Mason to serve thirty years before being eligible for parole. Mason didn't want the deal. He preferred death to life in prison.

His attorneys enlisted my help. They said I knew from personal experience what Mason was going through. All they wanted was for me to show Mason that there were other options to the almost certain death sentence.

The request tossed me on the horns of a dilemma. While I don't believe in the death penalty, I find it difficult to make a case for life imprisonment as an alternative. But after meeting with the attorneys and listening to their appeal, I agreed to speak to Mason so he would clearly understand his options.

Jail officials in Harris County didn't want to let me visit with Mason. His attorneys lobbied hard to secure the necessary official approval, even threatening to file a motion with the court to secure my access to the jail.

"Keep an eye on that sonuvabitch," the shift supervisor instructed a lower-level jail official as I stood in the jail's lobby with an investigator for one of Mason's attorneys. "If he gets out of line in any kind of way, lock his ass up."

It was the same treatment I had endured for so many years at the hands of Louisiana prison officials. It brought back harsh memories. I walked out of the jail, returning only when the attorney's investigator agreed to stay with me while I talked to Mason. I needed a witness to protect me from the retaliation that was coming if I said anything the guards could twist into a charge to revoke my parole.

The investigator, who came from England, sat outside the inmate visiting cubicle. She saw Mason as a human being who had tremendous potential to do good work even in prison.

Mason was easy to talk to. He's a convict — a designation that inmates reserve for prisoners tough enough not to knuckle under to prison authority. The nature and number of his tattoos confirmed a prison gang affiliation. I addressed him in convict language — straight and frank, no bullshit.

"I'm not here to sell you packaged goods, Bobby," I said. "There's nothing easy about a life sentence, or a death sentence. I know. I had both. I survived the death sentence, but there were a lot of times I wished I had let the Man kill me in the electric chair. I've never looked at life without parole as a merciful alternative to the death penalty. I've debated death penalty opponents who think life sentences are merciful."

Robert Mason measured his words carefully before speaking.

"That's my problem, man," he said. "I don't want to wake up one morning ten years down the road and realize I'm never getting out — you know, that I am going to die in a prison hellhole. I've already served sixteen fucking years and now these lawyers want me to start a life sentence."

"You can go to the bank that that day will come," I assured him. "It will come over and over. But you're a convict, Bobby — you've got balls between your legs. You're not a sniveling, ass-sucking inmate. You'll find a way to get up, pull that jumpsuit on, lace up those brogans, and get on with the fucking day, somehow, someway. It takes character, my man, to fight a life sentence. I've seen many succumb to it. They prefer being institutionalized to dealing with the struggle for survival. And it will always be hard for you because you'd rather have the Man's foot in your ass than his pat on your head."

A smile of understanding surfaced, exposing good, clean teeth. Mason definitely had character. He was clean-shaven, and his hair was neatly trimmed. He looked me straight in the eye. He wasn't a boot-licking inmate, and, more to the point, he was prepared to die.

"But let me tell you this, Bobby," I continued. "The Man will come to your cell on death row sure as the sun rises and sets, handcuffs and shackles in hand, telling you, 'It's time.' That's what the motherfucker wants — he's the Man; he represents the system. He's not just 'doing his job.' He's there to help kill you. He's an integral component in the death machine. He will strap you to that gurney and guard you till your last fucking breath, and he'll take a perverse pleasure in watching you die. He will celebrate your execution as much as crime victims will. Your execution is what the system wants, and that motherfucker with the handcuffs and shackles is there to fulfill those desires. He's a whore for the system, man."

Our eyes locked. Guards were watching us from the control center.

"But that's what I want, Billy," Mason said. "I don't want to live around them, or under them, for the rest of my life. I don't want them to have that kind of control over my life. I've had sixteen years of that shit. I'm thirty-six years old — I'll be *sixty-six* before I'm even eligible for parole, and you know what my chances for parole will be then. Fuck, man, you know what it's like. How can you ask me to take that, to give up, to plead fucking guilty to a sentence that's going to put me in that situation. Man, don't ask me to do that."

"I'm not asking you to do that, Bobby," I said. "What I'm telling you is this: Don't give the Man a victory; don't give him the satisfaction of giving you the death sentence and taking your life in that little room with those needles in Huntsville. You have the power to deprive the motherfucker of that satisfaction. You have the power not to let the system, and all those uniform-wearing motherfuckers who enforce it, have the pleasure of seeing you put to death."

The guard signaled that the visit was coming to an end.

"Listen to me," I said. "I'm not telling you to take that life sentence. What I am telling you is this: Don't give the Man the fucking pleasure of killing you. Don't let that asshole have that pleasure. You don't have to do that life sentence. You know that. If you ever reach a point where you can't do it anymore, get out of your bed one night, and walk to the dorm pisser. Just sit down on one of those stinking-ass toilets, and quietly slit your throat with a razor blade. That's your real power, Bobby. You have the power to deny the Man an opportunity to execute you, and you have the power after that to step out of that life sentence anytime you choose."

The guard's voice bellowed over a squeaky intercom, "Visiting time's over, Mason."

We both stood up. Mason put his fist against the scarred glass that separated us. "Thanks for coming, Billy."

I nodded. "Think about it," I said before walking away.

Mason did think about it. He pled guilty to the lesser charge with the life sentence two days before his death penalty trial was set to begin.

Bobby now controls his own destiny. Had he elected to go to trial in Houston, he would have been convicted, sentenced to death, and executed. When he was nineteen years old, Bobby took money to kill a man. It was a certain death penalty crime. And his certain execution would have been as banal as Ivon Ray Stanley's — except that the guards' celebratory remarks would not be on the Internet for the curious and the horrified to hear.

Texas lies at the epicenter of the death penalty. It worships killing. It has executed mass murderers with the same zeal it has executed inmates like Gary Graham, Todd Willingham, and Reuben Cantu, who had credible evidence of innocence develop in their favor before their executions. It has also executed more than its share of the mentally disturbed and put to death nearly two dozen more inmates whose cases a federal court never reviewed. Through the state's law of parties, it has even executed inmates who didn't kill anyone.

But it defied all the rules of legal logic and human decency when it executed two men under the same prosecutorial theory: that each man fired the single fatal shot that killed the one victim.

No one ever disputed that Joseph Nichols joined Willie Ray Williams in the robbery of a Houston delicatessen in October 1980. No one disputed that Claude Shaffer was shot and died during that robbery.

The prosecutorial theory after Williams and Nichols were arrested was that both men fled the store after the robbery but that Williams returned and fired the fatal bullet that severed Shaffer's aorta as he crouched for safety behind a counter.

Williams confessed to investigators that he was the triggerman. He was convicted in January 1981 after pleading guilty and was sentenced to death. He was executed as the triggerman on January 31, 1995.

Nichols was tried separately six months after Williams. The prosecution alleged that, under the Texas law of parties, Nichols was just as culpable as Williams. This law allowed the jury to return a death penalty verdict against Nichols, even though he didn't fire the fatal shot.

While the jury believed that Nichols took part in the robbery, it couldn't reach a verdict on the issue of punishment — life or death. The presiding judge declared a mistrial.

The district attorney's office decided to retry

Nichols with an amazing twist. At Nichols's second trial, in March 1982, the prosecution alleged that Williams, who had already been sentenced to death for the store clerk's murder, had lied about being the triggerman and that Nichols was the actual triggerman. The prosecution persuaded Nichols's second jury to disregard Williams's confession, the very confession it had accepted when Williams pleaded guilty to killing the store clerk at his capital trial in January 1981.

The prosecutorial strategy employed at Nichols's second trial was a significant departure from that of a traditional law of parties prosecution. Many defendants have been prosecuted and convicted as a party to a criminal act, including murder cases where the state didn't know who committed the actual murder. That's the historical premise of the law of parties rule in capital cases: It allows the state to proceed against all parties no matter who pulls the trigger.

But in the Claude Shaffer case the state knew who fired the fatal shot. The district attorney's office had Williams's confession, his guilty plea, and death sentence as the triggerman in the Shaffer murder. That's why it was a stunning reversal when the district attorney's office announced it would retry Nichols as the triggerman in the Shaffer murder. It marked the first time that a state would try, convict, and secure a death sentence against two criminal defendants at separate trials with the same theory: that each had been the triggerman who fired the single fatal shot that killed the victim.

It was a callous and dangerous decision, undermining the historical jurisprudence that evolved under a rule that has served the adversarial fact-finding process of the legal system in a rational way for decades.

As Nichols awaited lethal injection in March 2007, the Harris County District Attorney's Office defended its prosecutorial strategy by pointing out that the Texas appeals courts had upheld his conviction. But that offers cold comfort to those who favor a fair and consistent application of the law. The appellate courts that upheld Nichols's conviction also upheld the capital conviction of a defendant whose attorney *had slept through critical portions of the trial*; upheld criminal convictions obtained in Dallas County where DNA evidence later exonerated scores of defendants; and have received instructions on many occasions by the U. S. Supreme Court about what the Constitution does and doesn't allow in capital cases.

Perhaps the most troubling ethical aspect of the district attorney's decision to manipulate Williams's confession is that, before it could be introduced into evidence at Williams's trial, the prosecution had to establish its voluntariness — had to show that Williams gave his confession to law enforcement authorities freely and without coercion. The district attorney's office vouched for the confession's reliability when the prosecution introduced it at the punishment phase, effectively telling the jury: "This is what happened. Willie Ray Williams killed Claude Shaffer. We know that because he told us he did it with his confession."

When the prosecution elected to repudiate, before Nichols's second jury, the reliability of the confession it had theretofore guaranteed, its decision was not only unethical but morally reprehensible. A confession cannot be reliable enough at one trial to send a man to his death but sufficiently unreliable at another to condemn a second man to death for the same murder. This two-triggermen-one-bullet theory offends the very notion of due process held sacred in our constitutional system for more than 250 years.

Beyond the legal travesty of his execution, the Joseph Nichols case is also a social and moral tragedy. The organized religious community in Harris County, black and white, did not have the moral courage to take a public stand against his execution. This was not a death penalty case in which the usual pro and con arguments about capital punishment were debated. The Nichols case was about the social obligation and moral duty owed to the community by its religious leaders to step forward and condemn the district attorney's total disregard for the rule of law.

The issue in the Joseph Nichols case, therefore, was not so much whether he deserved to live or die. The issue was whether the rule of law — the spirit and letter of the law of parties — should have been respected and honored by courts bound to uphold it. That issue rises above any other consideration.

The execution of Joseph Nichols shows how callous prosecutors in Texas can be. By executing inmates whose cases raise probable claims of innocence, deplorable instances of ineffective assistance of counsel, and proven examples of egregious prosecutorial misconduct, the state's death machine marches relentlessly on in its determination to be the death penalty capital of the United States.

A lot of Texans seem to relish that.

5

The Cocktail

On September 25, 2007, the Supreme Court granted certiorari in the case of Ralph Baze and John Bowling, two convicted double murderers, who challenged the constitutionality of lethal injection as administered by the state of Kentucky. Baze and Bowling sought review of a decision by the Kentucky Supreme Court in April 2007 rejecting the two men's argument that the state's method of administering lethal injection amounted to cruel and unusual punishment.

This "cruel and unusual punishment" debate has not garnered much sympathy in the South. Officials in Texas, for example, a state that leads the nation in executions with 425 since 1982, have dismissed the growing body of medical evidence that lethal injection actually produces *more* pain and suffering than other traditional methods of execution: electric chair, firing squad, gas chamber, and hanging.

In other quarters the evidence has been receiving sober consideration. Two years before the Supreme Court agreed to hear the Baze and Bowling case, the issue gained legal and social prominence when the British medical journal *Lancet* published a "research letter" that said inmates previously executed in the United States may have experienced awareness and physical suffering because they had not been properly sedated. The *Lancet* study and subsequent debate predictably came to the attention of death row inmates' lawyers, who swiftly made use of the findings in their appeals. One such was lodged in the case of Philip Ray Workman, who was scheduled to die by lethal injection in Tennessee's death chamber on May 9, 2007.

On August 5, 1981, Workman had robbed a Wendy's restaurant in Memphis. He forced all the employees and a customer into the manager's office, where he put the day's receipts in a bag.

Workman didn't know that one of the employees had set off a silent alarm. As the robber walked out of the fast food establishment, a police lieutenant confronted him. In the ensuing scuffle, Workman broke free, the lieutenant was fatally shot in the chest, and another officer was wounded. Workman escaped, but an extensive search led to his capture a short time later.

Tried, convicted of capital murder, and sentenced to death in 1982, Workman survived five execution dates. In his final appeal, he argued to a U.S. district court that he feared he would suffer physical pain during a lethal injection execution. The court, in a ruling that drew national attention, issued a temporary restraining order barring prison officials from carrying out the execution. But in the end, that order, too, was overturned. "I've prayed to the Lord Jesus Christ not to lay charge of my death to any man," Workman said in his final statement. Two minutes after the lethal injection of drugs commenced, he said: "I commend my spirit unto your hands, Lord Jesus Christ."

It had taken a quarter century to bring Workman to the death chamber in May 2007, and under newly revised executions procedures, it took the state of Tennessee seventeen minutes to kill him. That time could be measured. How much he suffered could not.

A lethal injection in the United States generally consists of three drugs: sodium thiopental, pancuronium bromide, and potassium chloride.

Sodium thiopental is administered first. It acts as an anesthetic, depriving the brain of oxygen and rendering the inmate unconscious. Pancuronium bromide then paralyzes the skeletal muscles, immobilizing the condemned inmate, preventing him from moving or speaking. Potassium chloride then stops the heart by depriving it of oxygen, literally suffocating the organ.

The Kentucky Supreme Court described the legal injection protocol that was put before the U.S. Supreme Court in the Baze/Bowling case this way:

> The protocol for lethal injection execution begins with the availability of a therapeutic dose of diazepam if it is requested. Diazepam, commonly referred to as Valium, is an anti-anxiety agent used primarily for the relief of anxiety and associated nervousness and tension. Certified phlebotomists and emergency medical technicians are allowed up to an hour to then insert the appropriate needles into the arm, hand, leg or foot of the inmate.

Three grams of sodium thiopental, commonly referred to as Sodium Pentothal, are then injected. This drug is a fast acting barbiturate that renders the inmate unconscious. At this level of ingestion the person is rendered unconscious for hours. The line is then flushed with 25 milligrams of a saline solution to prevent adverse interaction between the drugs.

Fifty milligrams of pancuronium bromide, commonly referred to as Pavulon, follows. This drug causes paralysis. The purpose is to suspend muscular movement and to stop respiration or breathing. The line is again flushed with 25 milligrams of a saline solution to again prevent any adverse interaction between the drugs.

Finally, 240 milligrams of potassium chloride is injected. This chemical disrupts the electrical signals required for regular heart beat and results in cardiac arrest. An electrocardiogram verifies the cessation of heart activity. A doctor and a coroner then verify the cause of death.

Attorneys for Baze and Bowling outlined a more elaborate protocol in their certiorari petition to the Supreme Court:

Kentucky carries out lethal injections by injecting the same three chemicals used by all states other than New Jersey that carry out lethal injections: 1) sodium thiopental; 2) pancuronium bromide; and, 3) potassium chloride. This tri-chemical cocktail was first adopted in Oklahoma and first used in 1982 in Texas.

Sodium thiopental is a short-acting barbiturate that begins to wear off almost immediately.

When sodium thiopental was first adopted as part of the lethal injection protocol, it was a state-of-the-art anesthetic. Since then, it has been replaced in surgical settings by propofol. Pancuronium bromide is a neuromuscular blocking agent that paralyzes all voluntary muscle movements, but has no impact on the ability to feel pain. It prevents a person from speaking, moving, or expressing any other outward signs of pain or consciousness, but is extremely agonizing in a conscious person as the inflicted person suffocates just as if he or she was drowning with weights on his or her body to prevent movement. Potassium chloride, otherwise known as road salt used to melt ice, is injected to cause cardiac arrest, but is excruciatingly painful in a conscious person.

When used in lethal injections, sodium thiopental serves the purpose of rendering the condemned inmate unconscious. Pancuronium bromide is supposed to stop respiration, and potassium chloride is supposed to cause cardiac arrest. Because potassium chloride stops the heart from beating, death can and would be caused without the use of pancuronium bromide — a drug that is not permitted to be used to euthanize animals. Other than to pronounce death, doctors are not involved in Kentucky lethal injections, and the chemicals are injected from a room adjacent to the execution chamber. . . .

At trial, it was established that Respondents had conducted no studies to determine what chemicals to use in lethal injections, but merely relied upon what other states had "successfully" used. Further, undisputed testimony from both the experts for Petitioners and the expert for Respondent established that, if pancuronium bromide was eliminated from the execution process, death would be caused without any additional risk of pain and suffering. This would lessen the risk of pain and suffering because it would make monitoring for consciousness substantially easier. Likewise, undisputed testimony established that sodium thiopental could be replaced with propofol, or that propafol could be used as the only lethal injection chemical. Eliminating pancuronium bromide would lessen the risk of pain and suffering because it would increase the likelihood that the inmate would be unconscious throughout the execution, and, if used alone, would mean that excruciatingly painful chemicals are not injected.

Finally, undisputed testimony established that potassium chloride could be replaced by another chemical that would stop the heart, such as Dilantin — a chemical that is less likely than potassium chloride to cause pain. Despite the fact that this undisputed testimony established that the risk of pain and suffering caused by the currently used trichemical cocktail was unnecessary because it could easily be avoided, the trial court and the Kentucky Supreme Court upheld the use of these chemicals.

Likewise, the Kentucky courts did nothing about Respondents' inability to maintain life if a stay of execution is granted after the first or second chemical was injected. When this issue was raised at the trial court, it concerned Respondents so much that they purchased a "crash cart" and guaranteed that a doctor would be available during executions to use the crash cart if a last-minute stay of execution is granted. While this appears to be an improvement and, on its face, might appear to resolve the problem, in reality, trial testimony established that it was the equivalent of a pitcher attempting to hide the emery board he used to scuff up the baseball.

At trial, Respondents provided a list of the chemicals and equipment contained in its crash cart. Respondents' expert, Dr. Mark Dershwitz, was asked about the equipment and chemicals, and informed the trial court that those items were insufficient to maintain life after the first or second lethal injection chemicals were injected. Dr. Dershwitz testified that medications to increase blood pressure and contract the heart, as well as insulin, neostigmine, and artificial ventilation are necessary to maintain life after sodium thiopental and/or pancuronium bromide have been injected into a person. As Dr. Dershwitz pointed out at trial, none of these medications are part of Respondents' crash cart. Despite the obvious deficiencies with Respondents' crash cart that render it utterly useless and incapable of maintaining life if a stay of execution is granted after the first or second chemical is injected, the trial court denied relief on this claim.

One author of the *Lancet* research paper was Leonidas Koniaris, from the University of Miami's Miller School of Medicine. Koniaris and his colleagues studied lethal injection protocols in Texas and Virginia, where nearly half of the 1,135 post-*Furman* executions (through November 30, 2008) have taken place. They discovered that medical technicians carrying out the executions in these two states had no training in anesthesia; that the executions were not monitored for anesthesia; and that there was no postexecution review.

The researchers also analyzed autopsy toxicology reports on 49 condemned inmates executed in Arizona,

Georgia, North Carolina, and South Carolina. These reports revealed that the amount of sodium thiopental was lower in the blood of 43 of these condemned inmates than is required for surgery; and, more disturbingly, that 21 of them had such low concentrations of the drug that it indicated an awareness of pain during the execution process. In other words, the condemned inmates probably suffered an excruciating death, experiencing horrendous pain as their hearts stopped.

The Tennessee/Kentucky three-drug chemical cocktail had come under increasing judicial scrutiny for its efficacy prior to the September 2007 decision by the Supreme Court to hear the issue. The *Lancet* study lent credence to this judicial scrutiny.

The Tennessee Department of Corrections issued its own report on April 30, 2007, describing its new lethal injection protocol. The report said a five-gram dose of sodium thiopental "reduces oxygen flow to the brain and causes respiratory depression." This level of barbiturate, according to the DOC report, quickly anesthetizes the condemned inmate's brain and provides a sufficient dosage by itself to produce death.

The Tennessee report stated that pancuronium bromide is a "muscle paralytic" that assists "in the suppression of breathing and ensure[s] death." The report noted that the 100-milligram dose of this chemical is also sufficient by itself to inflict death. This paralytic chemical is used not only because it reportedly hastens death but also because it "prevents involuntary muscular movement that may interfere with the proper functioning of the IV equipment" to create the "mistaken" impression of physical suffering.

Finally, the report said that potassium chloride, a

salt, interferes with heart function, resulting in "cardiac arrest and rapid death."

The Tennessee DOC report concluded with the finding that sodium thiopental, when administered properly, anesthetizes the condemned inmate before the other two chemicals are administered, ensuring the condemned feels no physical pain and therefore does not suffer.

This "three-drug protocol" utilized to put Philip Ray Workman to death was created by an Oklahoma medical examiner named A. Jay Chapman more than thirty years ago. Dr. Chapman was instrumental in the decision by the Oklahoma legislature to enact the law that made Oklahoma the first state to abandon the electric chair in favor of lethal injection as its official method of executing condemned inmates.

Since then a number of studies have criticized the Chapman three-drug protocol. As the Supreme Court petition for Baze and Bowling noted, even veterinarians no longer use pancuronium bromide to euthanize animals because the vets now understand it produces a painful death. There have also been reports of people who underwent surgery, effectively immobilized by paralytic drugs but not adequately sedated with sodium thiopental, who suffered extreme pain during surgical procedures.

Opponents of pancuronium bromide argue that there is no need for the chemical to be used in the execution process. They charge that it conceals valuable information from the public about the execution itself. In other words, it prevents an inmate from crying out in pain, just as those who underwent surgery without proper sedation couldn't cry out in pain to alert doctors that they weren't properly anesthetized. State officials counter that they need the chemical to prevent an inmate's involuntary muscular movement.

In Louisiana's former electrocution process, a 500-volt charge of electricity was administered to the condemned inmate for 30 seconds before being reduced. A second 2,500-volt charge of electricity was administered for one minute before being reduced. A final 500-volt charge of electricity was administered for 30 seconds before being reduced. It took two minutes to complete the actual execution. The vast majority of the state's executions were uneventful.

That's because the first charge of electricity into the brain immediately rendered the condemned inmate unconscious. He was almost certainly dead before the second 2,500-volt charge was administered. Common experience, and medical expertise, instructs that high voltage electricity knocks people unconscious and produces almost instantaneous death. It may not produce a pretty death the way lethal injection does, but it almost certainly produces instant death.

The electric chair death process was also much simpler than the current lethal injection death process. Louisiana's condemned inmates were escorted from a nearby holding cell, allowed to make a final statement to attending witnesses, and strapped in the chair in less than a minute. Altogether, the walk from the holding cell, final statement, placement in the chair, and the administration of three high voltages of electricity took from 5 to 7 minutes.

The lethal injection process, however, takes much longer. It imposes far more physical and emotional distress on the condemned inmate and the staff. Prisoners are strapped to the gurney at least an hour before the actual execution begins. Untrained technicians must probe and puncture for good veins in which to insert the needles. And even after the chemicals are administered, it can take from 8 to 25 minutes before the inmate is pronounced dead.

Philip Ray Workman was lucid enough to make a statement two minutes after the sodium thiopental was administered. The Tennessee DOC report said that five grams of sodium thiopental would induce immediate unconsciousness. But it didn't. Had he been put to death in the electric chair, he would have been dead seconds after the first charge of electricity hit his brain.

There is no humane way to kill a human being. Some conservative radio talk show hosts have said the issue of how condemned inmates die should not even be a topic of social debate. Nazi Germany, which believed that Jews were as criminal as individuals currently on death row in this country, shared the same philosophy.

The doctor who invented the guillotine sought a humane way to put people to death, but he was horror-struck when he saw how his invention was ultimately used in French society. Decapitation is so sudden that it may leave the brain alive for several moments to contemplate the severed body. Lethal injection will one day stand alongside the guillotine as a failed experiment in how to kill people humanely.

On April 16, 2008, a fractured Supreme Court made this a certainty when it upheld Kentucky's lethal injection protocol. The court agreed with the Kentucky district court judge's assessment that there "are no methods of legal execution that are satisfactory to those who oppose the death penalty on moral, religious, or societal grounds." But it ruled that when sodium thiopental is properly administered, the condemned inmate should be rendered unconscious immediately and not be susceptible to any pain associated with the injections of pancuronium bromide and potassium chloride. In reaching this conclusion, the court considered a number of safeguards utilized by Kentucky officials designed to reduce the possibility of pain during an execution:

- Between injections of the three drugs, the execution team flushes the IV lines with 25 milligrams of saline to prevent a clogging of the lines "by precipitates that may form when residual sodium thiopental comes in contact with pancuronium bromide."
- The IV catheters are inserted by "qualified personnel having at least one year of professional experience."
- A certified phlebotomist and an EMT "perform the venipunctures necessary for the catheters."
- The phlebotomist and EMT have one hour to locate "primary and secondary peripheral intravenous sites in the arm, hand, leg, or foot of the inmate."
- Personnel besides the phlebotomist and EMT are "responsible for mixing the solutions containing the three drugs and loading them into syringes."
- The warden and deputy warden "remain in the execution chamber with the prisoner, who is strapped to a gurney."
- An execution team "administers the drugs remotely from the control room through five feet of IV tubing."
- If either the warden or deputy warden determines through visual inspection that "the prisoner is not unconscious within 60 seconds following the delivery of the sodium thiopental to the primary IV site, a new 3-gram dose of thiopental is administered to the secondary site before injecting the pancuronium and potassium chloride."

- In addition to monitoring the effects of the thiopental, the warden and deputy warden also observe "for any problems with the IV catheter and tubing."
- A physician on standby will "assist in any effort to revive the prisoner in the event of a last-minute stay of execution," although the doctor by law cannot participate in the actual execution.
- An EKG "verifies the death of the prisoner."

The attorneys for Baze and Bowling had already conceded that if the safeguards worked as intended, the end result would be a humane death. But they argued that, even with the safeguards, Kentucky's lethal injection protocol created an "unnecessary risk" of pain. The Supreme Court rebuffed that argument, although it did state that if a condemned inmate could show that a state execution procedure created a "future risk of harm" and the state refused to adopt an alternative procedure, the protocol could be viewed as "cruel and unusual" punishment. This loophole gave some death penalty opponents a glimmer of hope, but the court added it would be "difficult" to regard any lethal injection protocol "objectively intolerable" when it is so "widely tolerated" in this nation.

The court closed its decision with a caveat to lower courts:

> A stay of execution may not be granted on grounds such as those asserted here unless the condemned prisoner establishes that the State's lethal injection protocol creates a demonstrated risk of severe pain. He must show that the risk is substantiated when compared to the known and available alternatives. A

State with a lethal injection protocol substantially similar to the protocol we uphold today would not create a risk that meets this standard.

How a society chooses to kill its wrongdoers reflects its conscience. Killing without remorse, whether by an individual or a state, is equally horrific. When a society can put human beings to death with drugs and chemicals that can inflict indescribable pain and suffering without any humane concern, then revenge has paralyzed its collective soul.

6

Slow and Agonizing

Some punishments are worse than the death penalty.

Two inmates at Angola, known as the Angola Two, suffered a terrible form of torture. They lived in solitary confinement for thirty-five years — longer than any prisoners in America. Both are black. Both, I believe, are innocent of the 1972 prison murder that sent them into the worst form of lockdown in the United States. I believe they are innocent because the real murderer confessed to me that he killed the twenty-one-year old white guard named Brent Miller, found stabbed to death in a prison dormitory.

The Prisoner Grievance Committee introduced me to Miller's real killer, an inmate named Irvin "Life" Breaux, in 1973. A New Orleans native, Life was serving a life sentence for killing another inmate who made homosexual advances toward him. Life was one of the many militants who had been placed in maximum security

lockdown in 1972, following Miller's murder. I chronicled Life's story and his violent death in an article entitled "A Prison Tragedy" published in the prison's
newsmagazine, the *Angolite*, in 1979. That article won
me the American Bar Association's Silver Gavel Award
the following year.

During the six months that I knew Life, we became
close friends. In July 1973 he and I integrated the Big
Yard at the state prison without a single incident of violence — no minor feat, considering that Angola was
known as the bloodiest prison in America.

It was then that Life told me he had killed Brent
Miller, adding that Miller was an inadvertent "casualty
of war." Life and a number of other black militants had
concocted a plan to simultaneously kill twelve well-
known black inmate snitches and make Angola part of
the national black militant political movement then
sweeping the American prison system and the nation.
Life and his inmate followers believed that the killings
would support the political efforts of State Representative Dorothy Mae Taylor, who was waging a high-profile
campaign to change conditions at Angola.

They stashed homemade knives they planned to use
in a locker in Pine One Dormitory, one "shank" for each
designated snitch. Life and two others were putting the
knives in a large, bulky prison jacket when Miller unex-
pectedly walked into the dorm. He saw the inmates and
their weapons and tried to run. He didn't make it out of
the dormitory. Life caught him and led the knife attack
that killed him.

I didn't know if Life's story was true. It might have
been no more than a boast. There was no proof. I said
nothing to anyone about it, just as he expected. We stood

as one against the Man back then. When Life died a few months later in a prison fight, rumor had it that his death was official payback for his role in Miller's killing. I didn't know how much credence to place in the rumors then, and I still don't.

In 2001, after the publication of my memoir *A Life in the Balance*, a supporter of Herman Wallace and Albert Woodfox, two of the inmates originally convicted and sentenced to life in prison for Miller's murder, contacted me. The supporter suspected that I knew something about Miller's killing because of my years at Angola and the role I had played in the prison's tumultuous history in the early 1970s.

I told the supporter what Life told me, although it was part of a past long buried in a mind that didn't want to revisit the issue. In 2001 guards in the Louisiana prison system were still angry about Miller's death, and I was locked in a bitter legal struggle to secure my freedom from that system. Louisiana had invested thirty years of effort to keep Wallace and Woodfox in filthy isolation cells, and I had nothing to gain by taking on yet another legal battle.

But I elected to give Scott Fleming, the Oakland attorney representing the Angola Two, a sworn affidavit with permission to use it in court proceedings in an effort to secure new trials for the two inmates. It chronicled my relationship with Life and what he told me about Miller's murder. Fleming sent me a copy of the trial testimony of the state's star witness against Wallace and Woodfox, Hezekiah Brown. After reading the testimony, I knew the Angola Two were innocent — or at least that the killing had not happened as Brown had sworn it did at the trial of the two men.

Beyond Wallace and Woodfox's probable innocence also lies the issue of their punishment. They had languished in maximum security lockdown cells for thirty-five years when, in August 2007, a U.S. magistrate ruled that such an extended solitary confinement amounted to cruel and unusual punishment:

> Being housed in isolation in a tiny cell for 23 hours a day for over three decades results in serious deprivations of basic human needs. With each passing day its effects are exponentially increased, just as surely as a single drop of water repeated endlessly will eventually bore through the hardest of stones. By 1999, these plaintiffs had been in extended lockdown more than anyone in Angola's history, and more than any other living prisoner in the entire United States, according to plaintiffs' evidence. The men, now in their 60s, do not, and have not for some time, presented a threat to the "safety, security and good order of the facility."

Wallace and Woodfox had endured a fate worse than death in the electric chair with their thirty-five years in solitary confinement before being released into general inmate population in late 2007. While the 1972 *Furman* decision prevented them from being sentenced to death, the state of Louisiana would subsequently exact from them a punishment that eclipsed the death penalty itself.

How did this terrible injustice happen?

The Angola Two started out as the Angola Four.

In April 1972, black militancy gripped the Louisiana State Penitentiary. New York's Attica prison riot and its murderous suppression had occurred just eight months earlier. Prisons across America were instantly transformed into cauldrons of political unrest. The term "political prisoner" attached itself to every stripe of inmate from petty thieves to rapists, and even to cop killers. This political awakening had brutal consequences; prison officials employed violence and racism in order to suppress it.

When Brent Miller was killed, forty-five other inmates and I sat on death row, waiting. We were waiting for the Supreme Court to hand down its landmark death penalty decision — a decision that saved our lives.

With the help of a young civil rights attorney named Richard Hand, I became the first prisoner in Louisiana to win a prisoners' rights lawsuit — one that changed horrible conditions on death row. My reputation in 1971 as an emerging jailhouse lawyer surged like an electrical pulse through the prison. I was the man with the plan, particularly to the black militants who wanted to wage war against the system any way they could.

Angola's black inmate population had grown exponentially as a result of President Nixon's war on crime waged with Law Enforcement Assistance Administration funds. This new inmate group hailed mostly from New Orleans. Some called themselves Black Panthers, and they had Huey Newton and Eldridge Cleaver aspirations. But white staff still ruled Angola, a sprawling 18,000-acre plantation.

Dorothy Mae Taylor was the first black person elected to the Louisiana legislature since Reconstruction, and she quickly became a radical voice in the state's political system. Louisiana had just elected its first truly liberal governor, Edwin Edwards, who rode the black vote

into the governor's mansion and appointed longtime
penal reform advocate Elyan Hunt as the first female director in the state's prison system. The Edwards election
and the Hunt appointment emboldened both Representative Taylor and the black inmates to challenge the status quo at Angola. So it only made sense that Taylor set
her sights on the penitentiary.

But the lawmaker forgot the sage political advice of
Earl Long, who once warned that "there are only two
things you don't mess with in Louisiana: LSU and Angola." Taylor's political interest in the prison ignited the
budding black militancy movement. The administration
reacted by locking up scores of black inmates in a brutal
maximum-security unit known as close custody restric-
tion (CCR). It sat directly above death row.

In the spring of 1972, Louisiana's death row inmates
were enjoying the benefit of outdoor exercise for the very
first time. The privilege had come about as a result of the
lawsuit I had filed in 1970 challenging conditions on
death row, including a lack of outdoor exercise. Being on
the yard each day gave me an opportunity to communi-
cate with inmates in CCR by hollering at their windows.
A group of those black inmates wanted me to help them
file a similar lawsuit challenging conditions in CCR.

I was willing to help. I was waging my own private
war with the system. Richard Hand had given me the
fifty-four-page legal memorandum he had filed in connection with the death row suit. It was brilliant legal
work, containing all the prisoners' rights cases of that era.
Prison security had warned me that I could keep the writ
only so long as I didn't share it with other inmates. Their
warning didn't deter me: I typed a copy of the memorandum and smuggled it to the militants.

They used the brief to prepare a federal lawsuit challenging CCR conditions. A copy of their lawsuit ended up in the hands of Deputy Warden Lloyd Hoyle before it could be filed. He reacted swiftly. He didn't want another lawsuit like mine in federal court, believing it would play into the hands and efforts of Representative Taylor, who was pushing for a legislative investigation into prison conditions.

Hoyle ordered all the black militants housed on what had become known as "the Black Panther tier" released into the general population of the prison. These militants hailed me as their hero — a white man who bucked the system to help them. They sent me a lot of "right on, comrade" messages. Hoyle and prison security, however, saw it differently. To them, I was a troublemaker. They hoped I would be one of the first inmates executed if the Supreme Court upheld the death penalty in *Furman*.

Then the killing happened.

Brent Miller was murdered on April 17, 1972, in Pine One, an all-black dormitory on the Big Yard. The prison administration went crazy. They imported dozens of local farmers — many with Ku Klux Klan ties — deputized by the local sheriff to assist in the prison crisis. Hundreds of black inmates, all designated as militants, were locked up in various maximum-security cellblocks with as many as five to a cell. Wholesale beatings and torture followed swiftly in an effort to find out who killed Brent Miller and why.

Within weeks, four black inmates were named: Wallace, Woodfox, Gilbert Montegut, and Charles "Noxzema Black" Jackson. The media quickly dubbed them the Angola Four. Rumor had it that they had been among the inmates released from CCR by Hoyle. Only one of them had — Montegut. But that didn't stop one of Miller's brothers, also a prison guard, from retaliating by throwing Hoyle through a plate glass window, permanently disfiguring him.

The Angola Four quickly dwindled. Noxzema Black turned state witness against the others. Gilbert Montegut, mentally handicapped and functionally illiterate, was found guilty of manslaughter. His handicap was so apparent that not even an all-white West Feliciana Parish jury could find him guilty of murder. He was convicted only because he was tried with Wallace and Woodfox. They received life sentences for their alleged involvement in Miller's killing. They remain in Angola to this day, although they are no longer in solitary confinement: Wallace with a life sentence and Woodfox awaiting a third trial after a 2008 federal court reversal of his second trial.

The Supreme Court struck down the death penalty in *Furman v. Georgia* later that June, sparing my life and disappointing prison officials who believed that, if I hadn't provided the militants with the legal memorandum, Hoyle wouldn't have released them and Miller wouldn't have died. In their minds, a legal memorandum led to Miller's death.

But Brent Miller didn't die the way Louisiana and the only alleged eyewitness, Hezekiah Brown, said he did. Brown was on death row with me for an aggravated rape conviction. He was a snitch on death row, he was a snitch on the Big Yard, and his name was on Life's hit list. Brown was a habitual liar. He not only embellished accounts of his life, he manipulated the truth to fit his particular need in any given situation. Brown's trial testimony against the Angola Two convinced me that Miller could not have been killed the way Brown said he was. I don't know if Life killed Miller himself, but I do know that Brown would have been killed if he had witnessed Miller's murder the way he described it.

Now a chief prosecutor in the Louisiana attorney general's office, John Sinquefield prosecuted Wallace and Woodfox on behalf of West Feliciana Parish. The following is a transcript of Sinquefield's direct examination of Brown:

Q. Hezekiah, I'm going to ask you to speak up just as loud as you can so that the people on the back row of this jury, the defense attorney, and everybody in this court can hear you, and I want you to speak up loud when you answer these questions.
A. Okay.

Q. State your full name for the record.
A. Hezekiah Brown.

Q. Are you an inmate at Louisiana —
A. That's right —

Q. — State Penitentiary?
A. Yes, sir.

Q. Now, Hezekiah, what are you presently serving time for at the Louisiana State Penitentiary?
A. Aggravated rape.

Q. Did you spend some time on death row?
A. That's right.

Q. How long were you on death row?
A. About, say, about six years, something like that. I don't know exactly what — how many days.

Q. Were you subsequently removed from death row?
A. Beg your pardon?

Q. Were you subsequently — did you get off of death row after the six years?
A. That's right. I got off on — on account of they excluded to the jury.

Q. All right. Now, let me ask you . . . , Hezekiah, is that the first time you'd been in the penitentiary?
A. No, sir, it's not the first time I been in the penitentiary. It's my fourth time.

Q. All right. Were you there before on another charge?
A. Yes, six years for attempted aggravated rape.

Q. All right, so you've got a bad record; is that right, Hezekiah?
A. That's right, I have.

Q. But you're here today to tell the truth; is that correct?
A. From the bottom of my heart.

Q. All right, Hezekiah, I'm going to direct your attention to the day of April 17th, 1972. It was a Monday. Where — what — were you at the penitentiary?
A. Yes, sir.

Q. Speak up.
A. Yeah, yeah, yeah, yeah.

Q. What dormitory did you live in then?
A. I lived in Pine One.

Q. In Pine One. Where was your bed in Pine One, your bunk?

A. I slept in, sleep in number 68 bed. That was the first bed as you comes in from the walk—

Q. Right.

A. —the first bed on the right as you're coming in.

Q. All right. Now, Hezekiah, did you have a coffeepot that you kept at your bunk?

A. Yes, sir, I did.

Q. Did you make coffee occasionally in this coffeepot?

A. I shore did, every day.

Q. And did sometimes the correctional officers come in to get your coffee?

A. Yes, sir. In fact, all of them on that walk would drink coffee.

Q. Did you heat it up and prepare it for them?

A. Yes, sir, I heated it up.

His testimony here about the coffee revealed to the all-white, all-male jury that Hezekiah was an Uncle Tom, what inmates called a dorm snitch. He watched everything that went on in the dorm: who was doing dope, who was strong-arming, who was fucking whom, and any other information officers needed to understand the various players. Hezekiah was what Angola's white guards crudely called a Stepin Fetchit nigger, a crucial element in understanding his testimony.

Q. What kind of coffeepot did you have?

A. I had a electric coffeepot, about a ten—about a ten-cup coffeepot, about a ten-cup coffeepot, something kind of like that.

Q. All right now, Hezekiah —
A. Yes, sir.

Q. — did you know a correctional officer by the name of Brent Miller?
A. Yes, sir, I did.

Q. How long had Brent Miller been at the penitentiary?
A. I think he'd been working there about four months, three or four months. I don't know. I'd say it was something like that there.

Q. What kind of a fellow was Brent Miller?
A. As far as I know, he was all right with me.

Q. Did you ever see him mistreat any convict out there?
A. No, I never did.

Q. Did he have a habit of writing them up often?
A. I just know him to write up one man in my dormitory, and the dormitory where he was with me was Pine One, and that was a boy by the name of Knowles. I don't know nobody else he wrote up.

Q. All right. Now, prior, that is, before this morning that we're talking about here, had Brent Miller got coffee from you before?
A. Yes, sir, every day. All the time he was there he drank coffee from me.

Q. Did Brent — did Brent Miller — did you see Brent Miller on the morning of April 17th —
A. I shore did.

Q. — 1972?
A. I shore did.

Q. Did he come into your dormitory?
A. Yes, sir, he shore did.

Q. All right. Now, who was in that dormitory when
   Brent Miller came in?
A. I was.

Q. Who else?
A. I didn't see no one else?

I note here that Hezekiah is creating the impression that he was alone in Pine One when Miller came in. It was breakfast time. Most of the dorm inmates would have gone to breakfast, true, but not all of them. Hezekiah slept in bunk 68, so his testimony indicates that all of the other sixty-seven inmates went to chow. There is no way that would have happened. At most, two-thirds of any given dorm went to breakfast. The prison never served food that made its inmates rush to the dining hall. More to the point, though, the stronger inmates made their "punks" or "slaves" stay in the dorm to make their beds, clean their living area, and make sure no one went into their space. And faction leaders always left a sentry or two in the dorm at all times to keep a watch not only over their living area but also over their stash of drugs, money, and weapons. Faction leaders never, *ever* left a dorm unattended. It was precisely because an Uncle Tom like Hezekiah could be in a dormitory that the faction leaders left someone there to watch him. Just as Hezekiah watched everything in the dorm to collect information, the faction leaders watched him or had someone watching him to limit the amount of information he could gather to pass on to prison officials.

Q. For what purpose did Brent Miller come in there?
A. Come in there to get some coffee.

Q. All right. Did anything happen after that?
A. Yes, sir, it did.

Q. Now, Hezekiah, I want you to speak up as loud as
   you can, and I want you to tell this jury what you —
   what happened out there.
A. Well, that's what I want to do, but first I want to ask
   you, Judge, and all of y'all here: I want to have a few
   words, if I possibly can.

Q. Well, Hezekiah, I'd like for you, first of all, right now,
   of course, you have an opportunity to explain any answer to anything you want in here in this court today.
A. I know —

Q. All right. Now —
A. — but I got to say this —

Q. All right, say it.

GARRETON: Your Honor, I want to object. I don't
want Mr. Hezekiah Brown to make any opening statement to the jury, I want him to answer the statement or
question and explain if an explanation is due.

JUDGE: The answer must be responsive to the question.

Q. All right. Hezekiah, let me ask you this —
A. All right —

Q. Did you see Brent Miller get killed that day?
A. I shore did. I saw him get killed. Do you want me to
   go on and tell it?

Q. I want you to tell it just exactly like you saw it.

A. Well, that morning — I don't know when we got up that morning, but we got up to go to the lunchroom, you know, to go to breakfast that morning. Well, I don't know what happened, but they went to the dining room. I wasn't — I never did hardly ever go to the dining room for to eat, I always had something in my box there that I got from the commissary or places like that, and I sat there, and I had my coffeepot. Well, every morning around six o'clock I have the coffee on and have it hot, you know?

JUDGE: Talk into the microphone.

A. I have it hot and — [referring to microphone] that thing ain't right.

[Deputy Sheriff Rivet holds up the microphone for Brown to speak into.]

A. [To Deputy Sheriff Rivet] I'll hold it. Turn it a-loose. Now. So that morning when we — when they went to breakfast that morning, I don't know what happened at the dining room. I'm the orderly there, and so I got my broom and went on down around there and started to cleaning up. And after a pretty good while later they come in, all of them come back from the dining room into the building. Well, I put the broom down and went on back to my bed, you know? So when I went back to my bed, I remember sit — I sat down on my bed there a while to drink me another cup of coffee, and so I pulled the plug out, out of my pot, you know? Well, that made the coffee go, you know, get cool. So after a while the whistle blowed again for them to go back to the dining room.

86

Well, they went back to the dining room, and after they go back that left Mr. Miller at the — on the dormitory. Well, you see, they have two mens on the dormitory, you know, one go to the dining room with the men to feed them, and one stays on at the dormitory. So Mr. Miller was to stay. He stayed in the dormitory, and Mr. Hunter, he went to the dining room. So I don't — didn't know what happened then, but after a while all of them, all of them, after all of them cleared out, you know, all the inmates and everything, well, Mr. Miller, he come to the door and he called me. He said, "Brown," he said, "look," he says, "you got any coffee?" I say, "Yes, sir, I got some," I says, "but I don't think it's hot like you like it," you know? I said, "But you can come in, and I'll heat it up." So he came in, and when he came in he sat down on the side of my bunk, going to wait, just like this [illustrating].

Q. Which way was he facing, Hezekiah?
A. Well, just like it is right now, you know?

Q. Where was his back in relation —
A. Well, I'm going to —

Q. — to the door?
A. — I'm going to show you now. Well, he set catty-cornered just like I'm sitting here, and me and him was talking, but he was laying up on my bed just like this here, about on a forty-five angle, you know, like this-a-way with his back halfway to the door and his face toward me, you know?

Q. The door would be in the direction I'm sitting now?
A. That's right.

Q. All right. Go ahead.

A. So behind that, he — I was hooking up the coffeepot. By me a-hooking the coffeepot up, it was after a while, me and him was rapping, you know, talking about they had a wrop-out, it was that Saturday, you know. We — I had seen him out there on the rockkoppy, and he was, you know, shaking and dancing with them, you know. So me and him was talking about it and I says, "You was out there having a good time," you know? He says, "Yeah," he said, "that was real nice, Brown." He said, "It shore was." Then about that time, looked up — I heard some scuffling. I looked up there, and Fox throwed his arm —

Q. Who's Fox?

A. That's Fox right there, man, that's Fox right there.

Q. Had you known Fox before this?

A. Had I known him? I done been on the walk with him occasionally since I been over there, you know?

Q. So you'd know him when you'd see him?

A. Did I know him?

Q. Yes.

A. I'd know him if I was blinded; if I was blindfolded, I'd know Fox, shorely.

Q. Do you see him?

A. That's him right there [indicating], that's Woodfox. They call him Woodfox. I don't know his name, but we been calling him Woodfox ever since I been in that dormitory.

Q. Go ahead with what happened.

A. And I looked up. There was Fox, Hooks, Montegut and Noxzema Black. His name was Jackson is what it was, Jackson, but I forget all the name and call him by nickname, which was Noxzema Black. They came in about, oh, it was at the end of the bed, and he caught Mr. Miller about this-a-way [indicating] with his neck just like this, and he jobbed him when he rared him back. He rared him back on the knife.

Q. Now, wait, let me — I didn't understand, Hezekiah. Who grabbed — this was Mr. Miller who was grabbed?

A. Yes, sir. This thing here [microphone] worries me. Fox, Fox did it. He grabbed the man behind the neck, this-a-way. Let me show you. It was just — I don't know what hand, but just say right that-a-way, and he grabbed him and the man didn't say a word, you know? And he hit him in the back with that knife [illustrating throughout].

Q. Did you see —

A. Did I see it! I was standing as close to it with this man here [indicating Deputy Sheriff Rivet] as I am right here.

Q. Woodfox stabbed him with a knife?

A. He stabbed him, and then the rest of them grabbed him, and they started stabbing him. They picked him up off'n my bed and carried him into the, you know, into the — lavatory there — not the lavatory. You know what it is; the playroom by the cooler, and they was steady jooging on him then, you know?

Q. When you say "jooging," what do you mean?

A. That, that means a-stabbing him, hitting him.

I find this testamony unbelievable. Hezekiah said Woodfox stabbed Miller first while the guard was sitting on the inmate's bunk before the rest joined in the assault. Yet authorities found no blood on Hezekiah's bunk, on him, or in the immediate vicinity of his bunk. Stab wounds quickly produce copious amounts of blood, and with four inmates stabbing one officer, blood would have splattered everywhere in the vicinity.

Even more unbelievable, though, is Brown's testimony that the inmates attacked Miller on Brown's prison bunk, right under Brown's eye. Had those four inmates attacked Miller in the presence of a known snitch, they would have killed Brown, too. You don't kill a guard in front of a snitch and let the snitch live so he can rat you out.

Killing a prison guard is the worst crime an inmate can commit, worse even than killing a cop in the free world. No inmate would dare kill a guard in the presence of any other inmate, much less a snitch. In fact, four inmates taking part in that kind of killing would inevitably produce a state witness, and all prisoners knew that.

The rest of Brown's testimony is little more than irrelevant rambling. But Louisiana hitched its wagon to this Uncle Tom, and Sinquefield took him through the killing description several more times to make sure the jury got the picture. His testimony led to the convictions of Wallace and Woodfox.

I will never know if Life killed Brent Miller. If Wallace and Woodfox did take part in Miller's killing, Hezekiah Brown did not witness it. Louisiana's case against Herman Wallace and Albert Woodfox is based on a lie. It was a lie in 1972, and it remains a lie today.

And they paid an enormous price for that lie. Thirty-five years in solitary confinement is far more cruel and unusual than execution. No other inmates in modern American penal history have ever suffered such a slow and tortuous punishment.

7

Mistakes in Last-Minute Appeals

Last-minute appeals for a stay of execution — inevitable in death penalty cases — form part of the death drama. It is heightened when efforts to stay the executions are bungled and the executions proceed under questionable circumstances. An examination of two prominent cases will show that not much has changed in the last fifty years.

CARYL CHESSMAN

According to Alan Bisbort in his Gadfly Online article "The Curious Case of Caryl Chessman," on Sunday, May 2, 1960, the world-famous death row author was scheduled to be put to death in the gas chamber at California's San Quentin prison at 10:00 A.M. The infamous Red Light Bandit had spent more than twelve years fighting off his appointment with the executioner. At the time, that was the longest period a condemned inmate had spent on an American death row. Chessman's books and writings had attracted a league of international supporters, and his ability to avoid repeated dates with the executioner, together with his fame as a writer, focused the eyes of the world on California that May morning.

At 8:00 A.M., the California Supreme Court had assembled to hear a scheduled last-minute appeal from Chessman's attorney, George Davis. It came, and the judges rejected it by a 4–3 vote. At the same time the court was denying the appeal, French actress Brigitte Bardot was in the office of Governor Pat Brown unsuccessfully lobbying for a last-minute reprieve for the celebrated prison author.

Davis then rushed to the chambers of U.S. district judge Louis Goodman in San Francisco with a request for a stay based on newly discovered evidence. Two freelance journalists writing for *Argosy* magazine had reportedly uncovered the identity of the real Red Light Bandit, the attorney told the judge.

While Davis was pleading for a stay before the reluctant Judge Goodman, Celeste Hickey, the judge's secretary, entered the office to inform Goodman that Justice William O. Douglas had just announced that he would not intervene in the execution. Douglas had previously stayed an execution date for Chessman. The radio announcement that he would not intervene in the latest execution date made Judge Goodman even more reluctant to grant Davis's plea for a last-minute stay. It was 9:30 A.M.

Davis persisted. "Please, Judge, just let us give you an overview of what these two men have uncovered. It could save an innocent man's life."

Media accounts say the attorney reminded Goodman they were running out of time.

Several minutes before 10:00 A.M., Warden Fred Dickson escorted Chessman out of his death cell and led him into the gas chamber, where he was strapped into a chair.

"All right," Goodman told Davis, "I'll give you one hour. That's all." Judge Goodman then turned to his secretary. "Call Warden Dickson at San Quentin," he instructed. "Tell him to delay the execution for one hour on my order."

Hickey rushed out of the judge's office to her desk, but couldn't locate the prison's telephone number. While she was frantically trying to find it, at 10:00 A.M., the gas chamber was sealed. Three minutes later, Dickson signaled for the executioner to release the cyanide tablets into a vat of acid below the chair in which Chessman was restrained. The chamber began to fill with fumes.

As Chessman held his breath, the telephone in the death chamber rang.

Assistant Warden Reed Nelson answered it, learning from Hickey that Goodman had stayed Chessman's execution.

"It's too late," Nelson said. "The execution has begun."

The chamber was already permeated with the deadly cyanide fumes. Chessman vomited his breakfast, defecated, and died.

MICHAEL WAYNE RICHARD

A legal travesty like the one in Chessman's case sent Michael Wayne Richard to his death in the Texas death chamber on September 25, 2007, at the state's prison in Huntsville forty-seven years later. Richard was the only inmate in the nation scheduled for execution that day — the very day, as it happened, that the Supreme Court granted certiorari in the case of Ralph Baze and John Bowling, who had challenged the constitutionality of lethal injection as administered in Kentucky.

The Supreme Court's action that morning paved the way for Richard's attorney, David Dow, to seek a stay of his client's 6:00 P.M. execution. Dow, who runs the Texas Innocence Network at the University of Houston Law Center, and others began scrambling to prepare a 108-page petition in support of the request for a stay.

The clerk's office for the Texas Court of Criminal Appeals closed at 5:00 P.M. That, therefore, is the filing deadline. The court had a strict policy against late filings. Richard's legal team knew of this policy, adding urgency to their desire not only to get their legal documents filed timely but to allow time to submit a stay request directly to the Supreme Court should the state request be denied.

Judges with the Court of Criminal Appeals had anticipated a stay request in the Richard case. Judge Paul Womack stayed late at the court for just that reason. "It was reasonable to expect an effort would be made with some haste in light of the Supreme Court [action in the Baze case]," Womack told the *Houston Chronicle*. "It was an important issue. I wanted to be sure to be available in case it was raised."

Judge Cheryl Johnson had been assigned to handle

any late motions by Richard's attorneys. She was present at the court to entertain those motions.

Judge Cathy Cochran left the court early, but only because she knew other judges and court personnel were on hand to deal with the Richard case. "A number of judges stayed very late that evening, waiting for a filing from the defense attorney," Cochran told the *Chronicle*. "I would definitely accept anything at any time from someone who was about to be executed."

Then the unexpected happened. The computers used by Richard's attorneys to prepare that 108-page petition crashed. By the time they resolved the glitch, attorneys realized they couldn't meet the 5:00 P.M. deadline. Dow called the clerk's office and, according to the attorney, informed "someone" in the clerk's office about the computer problem and requested that the clerk's office stay open for an additional twenty or thirty minutes.

The "someone" in the clerk's office reportedly informed Chief Judge Sharon Keller about Dow's request to keep the clerk's office open for the additional period. Without consulting with the other judges — including Judge Johnson, who had been assigned the Richard case — Judge Keller refused to extend the 5:00 P.M. filing deadline.

It is unclear from the public record whether Richard's defense team attempted to secure a stay from the U.S. Supreme Court at that time. The *Chronicle* reported that "lawyers said that without a ruling by the Texas Court of Criminal Appeals on Richard's appeal, the U.S. Supreme Court couldn't consider it."

"I'd like my family to take care of each other," Richard said before his death. "I love you, Angel. Let's ride. I guess this is it." He was executed as scheduled and pronounced dead at 8:23 P.M.

In the wake of the Richard execution, Judge Keller came under both state and national fire for her refusal to extend the filing deadline.

"You're asking me whether something different would have happened if we had stayed open," Keller told the *Chronicle*, "and I think the question ought to be why didn't they [Richard's attorneys] file something on time? They had all day."

Dow called Keller's reasoning outrageous. Keller defended her position, saying that the lawyer did not give a reason for the request for more time. Dow disputed this, saying that he informed the clerk's office about the computer problem.

Jim Harrington, director of the Texas Civil Rights Project, quickly criticized Keller for refusing to extend the filing deadline. "When I saw that, I think I would just describe my reaction as 'stunningly unconscionable.' There has to be some kind of accountability for this," he told the *Chronicle*.

Judge Johnson, who was assigned to the Richard case, said she learned about Keller's decision from the *Austin American-Statesman* and was in "utter dismay." "And I was angry," she told the *Chronicle*. "If I am in charge of the execution, I ought to have known about these things, and I ought to have been asked whether I was willing to stay late and accept those filings."

There was certainly enough criticism to go around. Faced with a strict 5:00 P.M. deadline, why would the Richard defense team prepare a 108-page petition for a stay? Even if the petition had been timely filed before the 5:00 P.M. deadline, none of the judges could have digested a 108-page legal memorandum. And given that the Court of Criminal Appeals had already addressed and rejected previous constitutional claims that the lethal injection protocol violated the cruel and unusual punishment provisions, there was no need to swamp the court with a voluminous petition rehashing the same arguments.

Richard's defense team should have focused on speed and brevity before the state appeals court, standing ready to apply to the U.S. Supreme Court for a stay upon the probable denial by the state court. They lost precious time not only in preparing the ponderous legal brief but in printing out and assembling the requisite eleven copies needed for filing in the state appeals court.

The defense team should also face criticism for not contacting Judge Johnson directly. Dow said he spoke to "someone" in the clerk's office and informed that "someone" of the computer problem. At 4:30 P.M., the question Dow should have asked the clerk's office was the name of the judge assigned to the case. As soon as the computer crashed, the attorney should have requested a telephone conference with Judge Johnson, during which he could have asked for an extension of time to file the stay. There was more than a reasonable probability that she would have granted that request and ordered the clerk's office to accept any late filing by the defense team.

The misjudgments of the defense team notwithstanding, Judge Keller's refusal to extend the deadline was, to say the least, callous and "stunningly unconscionable."

"I think it's probably reflective of her own personal bias in this case about capital punishment and her lack of respect for the rights of defendants, the rights they have under the Constitution," Harrington told the *Chronicle*.

Chronicle columnist Rick Casey said of her, "Sharon Keller, Texas' top judge on criminal matters, may have shocked much of the nation . . . when she ordered a clerk not to stay open an extra 20 minutes to accept a last-minute appeal for a man on death row.

"But she didn't shock those who know her."

Twenty Texas lawyers filed a formal judicial misconduct complaint with the Court of Criminal Appeals against Keller in the wake of the Richard execution. The complaint, according to press reports, accused the state's top judge of violating the executed man's constitutional rights.

"Judge Keller's actions denied Michael Richard two constitutional rights, access to the courts and due process, which led to his execution," the complaint states. "Her actions also brought the integrity of the Texas judiciary and her court into disrepute."

The complaint was signed by Broadus Spivey, former president of the state's bar association; Houston criminal defense attorney Dick DeGuerin; University of Houston law professor Mike Olivas; former appellate judge Michol O'Connor; state representative Harold Dutton; and former Nueces County attorney Mike Westergren.

Texas attorney general Greg Abbott also came under fire. Two former Texas attorney generals, Mark White and Jim Mattox, took him to task publicly. White charged that Abbott, as an officer of the court, "should have been obligated to ask for a stay" of Richard's execution.

Pointing out that he once ordered an execution halted over objections of prison officials because he knew a reprieve would be issued, the recently deceased

Mattox had said, "When the state is all powerful, the state has got to be cautious in how it uses its power. Sometimes you do things not to protect the individual but to protect the system itself."

Michael Wayne Richard accomplished more in death than he could have ever imagined. His execution stirred the death penalty debate beyond the constitutional issue of whether lethal injection inflicts unnecessary pain and suffering on condemned inmates. The mishandling of the request for an extension of the filing deadline by Judge Keller brought to the fore the mean-spirited, biased, and callous nature of not only those who advocate the death penalty but those who carry out the ultimate punishment as well.

The 423 persons executed in Texas since 1982 shockingly reveal that one state alone has executed 37 percent of the 1,135 people put to death in this country from 1977 through November 30, 2008. Such bloodletting not only breeds social disregard for the sanctity of human life but clearly fosters a judicial contempt for the constitutional rights of those facing execution as well.

8

Two Cases of Innocence

In 2000, a freelance writer named J. J. Maloney wrote an article entitled "Will DNA Evidence Revolutionize Criminal Law?" for *Crime* magazine, an online publication. His article was based on a 1996 U.S. Justice Department report, *Convicted by Juries, Exonerated by Science: Studies in the Use of DNA Evidence to Establish Innocence After Trial*. The Justice Department report examined the cases of twenty-eight men convicted of violent sex crimes, including murder, who had been released from prison after DNA evidence exonerated them.

Even as recently as ten years ago, innocent men faced a daunting task when trying to establish their innocence. Many states did not recognize DNA evidence; defense attorneys weren't willing to take DNA cases; there were no codified methods for routine DNA testing; many states destroyed all physical evidence after final appeals were exhausted; and few inmates had the resources to secure the independent DNA testing that courts would accept.

DNA testing has now revolutionized how criminal defendants are prosecuted and defended in the courts. DNA has eroded many of the traditional assumptions on which criminal convictions were sought and secured. Chief among them is the notion that eyewitness testimony is the best evidence in a criminal case. The credibility of the pointed finger in criminal cases is no longer sacrosanct, especially in rape cases. DNA evidence has demonstrated that "absolutely certain" eyewitness testimony is often wrong and that innocent men have suffered in prison for decades based on its mistakes.

Two cases in Louisiana demonstrate the problems inherent in eyewitness testimony. Romallis Stukes is a black man from New Orleans. Johnny McIntyre is a white man from rural Webster Parish in northern Louisiana. Both were convicted of aggravated rape. Both inmates were serving life sentences at the David Wade Correctional Center near Homer, Louisiana, a small town just ten miles from the Arkansas border, when I was housed at the prison between 1994 and 2004. Both were bright. Stukes was amiable despite his plight. McIntyre was bitter and antisocial.

I served as jailhouse lawyer for Stukes and McIntyre when we shared the same prison unit. As a jailhouse lawyer, I had examined countless court documents in countless cases of every type for more than thirty years as I sought to secure retrials for inmates. As a prisoner, I observed inmate behavior for virtually the same period in various prison settings: in general population, in protective custody, and on death row.

I read both Stukes's and McIntyre's trial transcripts.

I studied their court records. I interviewed both on many occasions about their cases. Because we lived in the same small unit, I had the opportunity to observe their behavior every day. Neither man ever exhibited a single characteristic of a rapist. Years of experience separating truth from lies led me to the conclusion that both are innocent. And their cases make a striking argument against the death penalty. They demonstrate how easily an innocent man could be put to death in this country.

Between 1973 and November 30, 2008, 130 inmates were released from death rows in twenty-six states because evidence of their innocence surfaced after their trials. More than 200 inmates altogether have been freed from the nation's prisons over the last two decades through DNA evidence alone.

The nation's criminal justice system — dangerously infected with an unbridled law-and-order-at-any-cost virus — sends scores of innocent people to prison every year because prosecutors knowingly fabricate evidence, suppress favorable evidence, or use perjured testimony to secure convictions.

In a September 2007 syndicated column for the *Washington Post*, Stuart Taylor Jr. and Brooklyn College history professor K. C. Johnson wrote about the need for soul-searching following the Duke lacrosse rape case:

> One night in jail. So concludes the Duke lacrosse rape case — rape fraud, as it turned out. The legacy of this incident should include hard thinking about the deep pathologies underlying the media sensationalism and the perversion of academic ideals that this fraud inspired.
>
> The 24-hour sentence was imposed on Mike Nifong, the disbarred former district attorney of

Durham, after a contempt-of-court trial last week for repeatedly lying to hide DNA evidence of innocence. His prosecution of three demonstrably innocent defendants, based on an emotionally disturbed stripper's ever-changing account, may be the worst prosecutorial misconduct ever exposed while it was happening. Durham police officers and other officials aided Nifong, and the city and county face the threat of a massive lawsuit by the falsely accused former students seeking criminal justice reforms and compensation.

But most of the innocent criminal defendants ensnared in prosecutorial and law enforcement misconduct don't come from wealthy upper-class families like the Duke lacrosse players. They hail from the ranks of the disadvantaged who spend years, even decades, behind bars before evidence surfaces that could establish their innocence. And while there is no absolute, unequivocal set of facts to support the claim, empirical evidence makes it plain that innocent men have been executed in the nation's death chambers since the Supreme Court reinstated the death penalty in 1976. There can be no doubt, by even the most hardened law-and-order conservative, that innocent people were executed during the heyday of capital punishment between 1930 and 1967 — especially among those 405 cases involving black men executed for raping white women.

The Case of Romallis Stukes

A large, robust man, easily six foot three and 280 pounds, Romallis Stukes is exceptionally intelligent and well read, versed in a wide range of subjects, particularly electronics. A good professional cop, he had only one blemish on his record, a minor incident in which he handled a suspect too roughly.

In the mid-1980s Stukes was going through a bitter divorce and custody battle with his former wife, a reputed heroin user. The couple had two children, a four-year-old girl and a ten-year-old boy. Stukes had received partial custody of the children and visitation rights. But, as in most divorce cases in Louisiana, his ex-wife enjoyed primary custody rights. The children spent weekends with Stukes, who had a neighbor care for them while he worked two extra jobs with security firms.

Stukes's wife had a sixteen-year-old babysitter care for the children. At his trial, Stukes's defense attorney sought to establish that the "sitter" was in fact a drug user who supplied drugs to Stukes's ex-wife.

It was the babysitter who discovered and reported the first evidence of the alleged rape. She was drying off the Stukes daughter after a bath when the child expressed discomfort as the towel was being rubbed against her genitals. The sitter questioned both children about whether their father had sexually abused them. Both children denied any abuse.

The babysitter and Stukes's ex-wife decided to take the children to a local hospital, where the attending physician, by law, had to report the matter to the New Orleans police. This time, the four-year-old told the detectives that Stukes had sexually abused her. The boy continued to deny any sexual abuse, but he changed his story after a police interview.

The only evidence presented by the prosecution at trial was the testimony of the four-year-old girl. She told the judge — Stukes had waived his right to a jury trial — that her father penetrated her, had sexual intercourse, and ejaculated some "green stuff" in the process. The prosecution also put the Stukes boy on the witness stand to rebut the ex-cop's testimony that he had never sexually abused his children. The son testified that his father had anal intercourse with him.

No physical evidence supported the children's testimony. Prosecution doctors had examined both and found no evidence of sexual abuse in either child. In Louisiana, the lack of physical evidence in a rape prosecution is immaterial. The testimony of the victim alone is sufficient to sustain a conviction.

The young girl's description of the alleged rape flies in the face of the doctors' examination. The four-year-old said a fully-developed male penis penetrated her undeveloped vagina. She then claimed her father engaged in actual sexual intercourse with her and that he ejaculated "green stuff." She did not testify about any pain, blood, bruising, or swelling caused by the rape, and the doctors' examination revealed none of the physical indications normally present when an adult male has sexually abused a child.

The same held true with the ten-year-old boy. Anal intercourse stretches the sphincter muscle, according to medical experts, and the doctors' examination of the boy found no evidence at all of anal intercourse.

While the testimony of a child about sexual abuse is compelling, courts simply cannot credit such testimony when no physical evidence supports it. The kind of rape described by Stukes's daughter could not have occurred without leaving physical damage detectable by doctors.

Stukes also never once gave the slightest indication

that he could, or actually did, rape his own daughter. Sex offenders give themselves away by an avid interest in abnormal sex, a predilection for pornography, and constant chatter about females in a sexual context. In my many conversations with Stukes, particularly during the period when I provided him with legal assistance, he never revealed an interest in any of these.

THE CASE OF JOHNNY MCINTYRE

I came to the same conclusion about McIntyre, a small-town, beer-drinking, pot-smoking troublemaker. He had married above his social status, and in his case it proved a horrible mistake. Histrionic fights, clothes thrown from a house trailer into the yard, and a pestering mother-in-law finally brought an end to his "redneck marriage," as he called it. But the marriage had produced a beautiful daughter, whom he loved dearly.

His mother-in-law, however, was determined that McIntyre wouldn't have a relationship with her granddaughter. She instructed her daughter to keep the child away from him. His repeated telephone calls, threats, and drunken appearances at his mother-in-law's residence created perpetual conflict between the estranged couple.

Finally, one night after hours of heavy drinking, McIntyre drove to the mother- and father-in-law's residence. Armed with a sawed-off shotgun, he demanded to know where his daughter was. The mother-in-law grew belligerent. After McIntyre hit his father-in-law on the side of the head with the barrel of the shotgun, his mother-in-law realized he meant business.

McIntyre kidnapped the couple, driving them from

their residence in Shreveport to his trailer in rural Webster Parish, where he interrogated them in an attempt to find his daughter. According to the mother-in-law's testimony at trial, McIntyre then tied up the father-in-law and took her into the bedroom, where he made her lie on the bed. She said he put the shotgun in a corner before getting in bed with her.

The mother-in-law testified that she was menstruating and that she had inserted a tampon into her vaginal canal to absorb the blood. She told the jury that McIntyre performed oral sex on her for forty-five minutes before raping her with the tampon still inside her.

Her own physician examined the mother-in-law on the night of the alleged rape. The physician told the jury that the victim was not unusually upset and that his examination had revealed no bruising, swelling, redness, or abrasions. No physical evidence supported the kind of sexual assault the mother-in-law described.

But the post-rape examination did find spermatozoa in her vaginal canal. Tests determined that the spermatozoa had been deposited in her vagina at least twelve hours before she claimed she had been raped by McIntyre. Examination also discovered a male pubic hair on the woman's body that did not belong to McIntyre. This physical evidence clearly established that the victim had had recent sexual intercourse — but not with McIntyre.

TESTS VERSUS TESTIMONY

The Louisiana rule of evidence that allows the crime of rape to be established solely through the victim's testimony easily creates miscarriages of justice, as the Stukes and McIntyre cases demonstrate. The alleged rapes in both cases could not have occurred as the victims testified under oath without leaving some physical evidence of the assault.

So why did the prosecutors in these cases take them to trial?

The answer is simple. Criminal convictions come easily in sex offense cases. They enhance a district attorney's crime-fighting reputation — a valuable asset in elections. It paid off for Nifong. He easily returned to office before proof of his duplicity reared its ugly head.

Political considerations also lurk behind prosecutors' negative reactions to the emergence of exculpatory DNA evidence. A commendable few prosecutors join with defense attorneys to see that exonerated inmates immediately go free, but most fight defiantly, refusing to accept DNA evidence.

This prosecutorial reluctance to embrace exculpatory DNA evidence played a role in the Gene Bibbins rape case in Baton Rouge in 2002. Bibbins was the first inmate in Louisiana to gain access to biological evidence for testing under the state's new DNA postconviction statute. DNA testing unequivocally established that he was not the man who raped a thirteen-year-old in 1986.

The victim had made a positive in-court identification of Bibbins at trial. That Bibbins had in his possession a radio belonging to the victim only bolstered the power of the in-court identification. The prosecution believed the case was a slam dunk. Bibbins, however, maintained his innocence, saying he found the radio in some bushes as he walked down the street.

When the DNA test results excluded Bibbins as the rapist, Assistant District Attorney Sue Bernie, reluctant to accept the findings, stood by the in-court identification made by the victim and the physical evidence provided by the radio. Bernie ultimately told the court she would not oppose Bibbins's court-ordered release, but, as Tulane University law professor Jancy Hoeffel pointed out after Bibbins walked out of prison, some prosecutors often believe they convicted the right person, regardless of what the court may rule.

Bibbins was the 125th person exonerated by DNA evidence in the United States, and his exoneration supported the 1996 Justice Department finding that as many as 20 to 25 percent of criminal defendants prosecuted for sex crimes are innocent. The first person exonerated by DNA evidence, according to the Cardozo School of Law's Innocence Project, was Illinois inmate Gene Dotson, who was freed in 1989 from a ten-year-old rape conviction.

In the wake of the Dotson exoneration, both Illinois and the federal government began compiling mandatory DNA databases. By the end of 2002, the FBI reported that nearly seven thousand DNA samples had been matched to unsolved crimes. Virginia alone had matched DNA evidence to 74 crimes, including 12 rapes and 9 murders committed by juveniles. Those numbers made prosecutors giddy.

But many of the same prosecutors sing a different song when DNA evidence reveals a wrongful conviction. Frank Jung, a Missouri assistant attorney general, went on record in 2003 before the Missouri Supreme Court suggesting that even if the court found there was actual evidence of innocence in the capital case before the court, the condemned inmate, who spent seventeen years on death row before being exonerated by DNA, should be executed anyway. Jung is part of a league of prosecutors who feel that claims of innocence should not be entertained by the courts after the trial and appeal in a criminal case. They believe that the criminal justice system's interest in the "finality of conviction" is more important than saving an innocent man from death.

Because of prosecutors like Jung, Bernie, and Nifong, the courts suddenly found themselves drawn into the growing DNA firestorm. This was evident in the Virginia rape case of James Harvey, who was convicted in 1990 and sentenced to consecutive terms of twenty-five years for rape and fifteen years for forcible sodomy. In 1998 and 1999, the inmate requested that the district attorney provide him with access to the state's physical evidence in his case so it could be subjected to DNA testing. The prosecutor refused. Harvey filed a civil rights lawsuit claiming that he had a constitutional right to the evidence. A local federal court agreed, ordering the state to produce the evidence.

The Fourth Circuit Court of Appeals, however, reversed the lower court's ruling. The appeals court made it clear that it was not prepared to extend a "constitutional" right to state inmates in the postconviction process, allowing them to have access to evidence that could potentially establish their innocence, no matter how compelling that evidence might be.

Shortly after the Fourth Circuit issued that decision, Peter J. Neufeld, a pioneer in the Innocence Project, testified before the House Committee on Crime, Terrorism, and Homeland Security concerning the Innocence Project Act of 2001:

> There are now 108 Americans who have been exonerated by postconviction DNA testing.

Thirteen of the exonerated had at one time been sentenced to death. Thirty-two of the exonerated were convicted of murder, and many of them would have almost certainly faced execution if the death penalty had been available in the jurisdictions where they were tried. Collectively, those 108 men have served 1,116 years in prison.

The pace of postconviction DNA exonerations has accelerated because states have begun to pass statutes that permit those claiming innocence a chance to gain their freedom. In 1993 there were three DNA exonerations. Thirty-five law schools have started a network of "innocence projects" on shoestring budgets to prevent, as best they can, these DNA statutes from becoming unfunded, unrealized mandates. There can be no doubt that the number of wrongly convicted freed by DNA testing would dramatically increase if postconviction DNA legislation were passed by this Congress — the number of exonerations would at least double within five years — just as apprehension of the real perpetrators of these crimes through DNA data-bank "hits" would impressively proliferate. This is a win-win proposition for law enforcement, for innocents who rot in America's prisons and on death row, for crime victims, for families of all involved, and for anyone who believes in justice.

At about the same time that Neufeld was testifying before Congress, the Associated Press was analyzing the data associated with the nation's first hundred DNA exonerations. The AP found that eleven of the exonerated men had been sentenced to death, half had no prior convictions, two-thirds were convicted through mistaken eyewitness testimony by either victims or bystanders, 14 percent were imprisoned through mistakes or misconduct by forensic experts, nine were either mentally handicapped or borderline handicapped and had confessed after being tricked or coerced by authorities, approximately two-thirds were either black or Hispanic — and about 60 percent had been aided by the Innocence Project at the Cardozo Law School.

What is particularly disturbing about the AP report is the finding that since 1989, when DNA evidence was first utilized in a criminal case, tens of thousands of individuals who were arrested or indicted were cleared prior to trial by DNA evidence. This finding also reinforced the 1996 Justice Department conclusion that as many as 25 percent of all convicted sex offenders are innocent. This disconcerting reality has prompted twenty-one states, the federal government, and the District of Columbia to enact legislation to compensate the wrongfully convicted. Other states have initiated reforms in their criminal justice systems as well.

In 2001, former New Jersey attorney general John Farmer Jr. wrote about the need for eyewitness identification guidelines in the wake of so many DNA exonerations: "It is axiomatic that eyewitness identification evidence is often crucial in identifying perpetrators and exonerating the innocent. However, recent cases in which DNA has been utilized to exonerate individuals convicted almost exclusively on the basis of eyewitness identifications demonstrate that this evidence is not foolproof."

New Jersey became the first state to adopt recommendations made by the U.S. Justice Department in its 1999 *Eyewitness Evidence: A Guide for Law Enforcement* by implementing safeguards in the state's eyewitness identification procedures. DNA exonerations made it absolutely clear to New Jersey officials that mistaken identifications are more prevalent than generally perceived.

In the May 3, 2007, edition of the *Washington Post*, Darryl Fears wrote about the two-hundredth person exonerated by DNA evidence, Jerry Miller, who spent twenty-five years in the Illinois prison system for a rape he didn't commit. He was the victim of a mistaken identification.

The 2007 DNA statistics cited by Fears continued to mirror the earlier Associated Press analysis: 60 percent of the two hundred exonerated inmates were black or Hispanic, and of those exonerated in rape cases, 85 percent were black men convicted of raping white women, although blacks are accused in only one-third of rapes of white women.

"What it says to me is that, ultimately, if you are a black man charged with sexually assaulting a white woman, the likelihood that you will be convicted, even if you are stone-cold innocent, is much, much higher," Peter Neufeld told Fears, adding that the two hundred exonerations "are the tip of the iceberg."

Fears wrote that DNA exonerations have resulted in the reversal of so many criminal convictions that it "is prompting changes in criminal procedures that reach beyond race. States and cities are starting to enact or consider laws to change decades-old police methods such as eyewitness identifications and police interrogations that lead to confessions."

Gary Wells, a psychology professor at Iowa State University whose research has contributed to recent changes in eyewitness identification procedures in that state, was quoted in the *Post* article: "The exonerations have been an extremely important force in getting the legal system to recognize there's a problem. I've been working at this for 30 years, and before DNA they pretty much ignored the studies."

DNA has also prompted some dramatic changes in policy and law. After DNA evidence overturned four convictions in New Jersey, the state's attorney general directed that all police interrogations in violent-crime cases be recorded electronically to protect against false confessions. The *Post* reported that the practice had been adopted by some five hundred police forces across the country and was under consideration in a score of states including California, Florida, Tennessee, and Virginia.

Former prosecutor and now U.S. senator Amy Klobuchar said that Minnesota started taping confessions more than a decade ago, following a state supreme court ruling. "Police and prosecutors I've talked to thought it was a good thing," she told the *Post*. "It builds police credibility. People talked about it being too expensive. But I would put buying a cheap tape recorder over paying some of these multimillion-dollar wrongful-conviction judgments any day."

The *Post* article also underscored that 75 percent of the DNA exonerations involved mistaken identification. The newspaper reported that New Jersey discarded its "old police lineup" practices that allowed victims and eyewitnesses to view criminal suspects in an array of photographs and then in an actual "in-person lineup" attended by investigating detectives who often provided suggestions about whom to identify.

New Jersey's new identification guidelines, set up by the attorney general's office, "now present individuals — in person or in photos — one after the other so witnesses cannot compare one member of a lineup to another, making relative judgments 'about which individual most looks like the perpetrator,'" reported the *Post*.

But not all law enforcement authorities agree with changing those procedures. "It's way far from being established that this is the magic bullet," said Joshua Marquis, district attorney for Clatsop County, Oregon, and vice president of the National District Attorneys Association. Cautioning against the new eyewitness procedures, he said they could set the guilty free, but he conceded prosecutors want "eyewitness identification that is valid."

Yet with so many wrongful convictions obtained through mistaken identification, it is difficult to refute the compelling need for nationwide changes in eyewitness identification procedures. For example, army veteran Jerry Miller was at home on September 1981 watching the classic welterweight title bout between Sugar Ray Leonard and Tommy Hearns. He had an alibi witness who watched the fight with him. Still, he was identified at a criminal trial as the person who committed a rape that night. Fortunately, the police preserved the evidence that ultimately led to his DNA exoneration. But it came a quarter of a century late.

In 1994, Jennifer Thompson sat in a North Carolina courtroom and apologized to Ronald Cotton, whom she had mistakenly identified as her rapist. In the *Post* article Thompson, who is white, described the eyewitness identification process in which she fingered Cotton, who is black:

> "When you sit down and look at the choices in front of you, the hundred noses, the hundred eyebrows, you try to get the best eyes, eyelashes, the

best lips," she said. "When the composite was finished and I was asked, 'Does it look like the man who attacked you?' I said, 'Yes, it looks like the man.' . . . I did get verbal and nonverbal encouragement: 'Good job. Way to go,'" she said. "In the lineup, I looked for somebody who looked like the photograph. And Ronald Cotton was doomed."

Cotton spent ten years in prison before securing a new trial. Thompson insisted at Cotton's second trial that he was the man who had raped her. Then the real rapist confessed, and DNA evidence supported his confession.

Beyond its challenge to victim eyewitness testimony, DNA evidence has also undermined prosecutorial "expert witness" testimony. Several of the twenty-eight cases reported in 1996 by the Justice Department involved the same "forensic chemist" who, as Maloney wrote, "testified at 130 (in several states) criminal trials before it was learned he had lied about his credentials and training, and in some cases had committed outright perjury concerning his actual findings."

The 1996 study, the first of its kind, came to a stunning conclusion based on 20,000 tests conducted in an FBI laboratory: "20 percent . . . revealed that the person charged with the crime was 'excluded' by the test — meaning the blood of the defendant did not match with the semen, blood, hair or other body cells found on the victim or at the scene of the crime," Maloney wrote.

The two most egregious examples of "expert" witness misconduct involved former West Virginia State Police sergeant Fred Zain and former Oklahoma City Police Lab director Joyce Gilchrist.

In Zain's case, the West Virginia Supreme Court

said that "any testimonial or documentary evidence offered by Zain, the West Virginia State Police sergeant,
at any time, should be deemed invalid, unreliable, and
inadmissible." The West Virginia high court pointed out
that Zain had even testified about tests that the police lab
didn't have the necessary equipment to perform.

The Zain episode resulted in wrongful or constitu-
tionally suspect convictions in many different jurisdictions. A Texas court of appeals found that Zain
committed perjury in the case of Charles Mark Tuffiash,
who was convicted for the 1990 murder of his wife and
sentenced to thirty years in prison.

The Oklahoma City Police Department hired Joyce
Gilchrist as a forensic scientist in 1980, and the South-
western Association of Forensic Scientists soon began receiving complaints charging her with misconduct. For
years the association refused to address the Gilchrist
problem, but it finally did rebuke her in 1987 for violating the group's code of ethics. The FBI reviewed 680 of
the thousands of cases Gilchrist had handled, finding "serious" concerns in 112 of them.

Not all the convictions obtained because of perjured
testimony by Zain and Gilchrist resulted in new trials. In
the Tuffiash case, the court of appeals simply returned it
to the trial court with instructions that he be granted an
out-of-time appeal. More specifically, the West Virginia
Supreme Court said that "although it is a violation of due
process for a state to convict a defendant based on false
evidence, such conviction will not be set aside unless it is
shown that the false evidence had a material effect on the
jury verdict."

Wrongfully convicted defendants, therefore, have a
double hurdle: they must establish that false evidence was

used; then, at a second hearing, they must show that the jury convicted them because of that false evidence. This rigid judicial double standard hardly squares with a meaningful public policy that protects innocent, law-abiding citizens from wrongful criminal conviction. Once a judicial decision determines that forensic misconduct has taken place in a criminal trial, the conviction should be reversed without a required showing of prejudice. That's the only way to protect the integrity of our adversarial system of justice, the primary objective of which should be to establish the truth in an orderly, lawful manner. A long-respected legal maxim once governed society: "It is better that ten guilty persons escape than that one innocent suffer," penned by Sir William Blackstone, the English jurist whose 1769 *Commentaries on the Laws of England* gives the best-known description of the doctrines and ideals of English law, which serves as the basis of American law. Today, that revered maxim has been inverted: "Better that ten innocent men be imprisoned than that one guilty go free. The others are likely guilty of something anyway." It's this kind of public sentiment, driven by fear, that has led to restrictive laws like the Antiterrorism and Effective Death Penalty Act, which severely limits state prisoners' access to the writ of habeas corpus in federal court even when there are compelling arguments of actual innocence, and the Detainees Fair Treatment Act and the Military Commission Act, which eliminated altogether access to habeas corpus and to any other form of judicial remedy for prisoners designated as "enemy combatants."

With laws like these, it is a certainty that the number of innocent people wrongfully convicted will increase dramatically — for being in the wrong place at the wrong time, having the wrong skin color, being mistakenly identified by a rape victim, or being the target of a vengeful wife or mother-in-law.

There is little hope that Romallis Stukes and Johnny McIntyre will die outside the Louisiana prison system. Their innocence will go with them to the grave in a prison cemetery. Prison medical records that record their deaths will ultimately be destroyed themselves. How many more Stukeses and McIntyres are out there?

In 1950, Englishman Timothy Evans was hanged for the murder of his child. He initially confessed to killing his wife but then retracted the confession. Investigators couldn't find the bodies of his wife and child. John Christie, a neighbor, served as the key witness for the prosecution. Four years after Evans was hanged, Christie confessed to murdering seven women, including Evans's wife and child. Investigators found the bodies of his victims walled up in his home. Christie was also hanged. It took Queen Elizabeth II more than a decade to pardon Evans posthumously, citing his innocence in her 1965 pardon.

The United States has faced compelling evidence that innocent persons have been executed since the Supreme Court reinstated the death penalty in 1976, but irrefutable evidence — like DNA testing or walled-up bodies — has yet to prove that an innocent person has died in a U.S. death chamber. When that finally happens, as it will, the United States may abolish the death penalty as England did following Timothy Evans's wrongful execution. If not, barbarism will rule a nation founded on the principle of justice for all.

9

Another Texas
DNA Exoneration

In May 1993, in Houston's Third Ward, a thirty-eight-year-old woman lay asleep in her home when a man put a knife to her throat. The intruder raped the woman and fled the residence. The victim called the police to report the sexual assault. Two police officers arrived at the scene an hour later. The officers identified a "wet spot" on the sheet where the rape occurred. The rape victim told the officers that she had felt the assailant's features during the attack but had gotten just a brief glimpse of him. The only light in the victim's residence came from a street-light across the street.

The police questioned neighbors about the incident. One neighbor recalled that she had seen Ronald Gene Taylor in the vicinity earlier in the night. Taylor lived less than a mile from the rape victim's home and had been living in the area for only six months, having recently moved there from Huntsville, Texas. The police went to his home, rousted him out of bed, and hauled him off to jail. They told him only that he had been accused of raping a woman.

Afterward, police could not locate the victim to view Taylor in a lineup, so they videotaped the men they had assembled for the lineup. A lone police officer then took the videotape to the victim's residence so she could view it. Taylor was not represented by counsel when officers assembled men for the lineup, nor were there any witnesses to it other than the officer who did the videotaping.

While viewing the video, the victim remembered suddenly that her assailant was missing a tooth. This information had not been part of her initial description of the assailant. She had told the two investigating officers that she had managed only a "glimpse" of her assailant before he fled. Taylor had a missing tooth. The victim promptly identified him as her assailant.

It is unclear from the public record whether the victim experienced this "sudden recollection" about the missing tooth before or after she viewed the videotape. What is clear is that the police investigation ended with the victim's identification of Taylor as her assailant. The case was closed as far as the police were concerned.

At the time of his arrest, Taylor was engaged to be married. His fiancée, Jeanette Brown, refused even to consider the possibility that the man she loved had committed such a crime. "I know that man, and I know he is not capable of doing something that awful," she told the local media.

Taylor's mother, Dorothy Henderson, was equally convinced of her son's innocence. "He always said that he was innocent, and I kept the faith that one day it would come through that it was not him," she told reporters.

Taylor believed in the criminal justice system at the beginning and maintained his innocence to anyone who would listen.

"Rape is one of the worst crimes you can do," Taylor said to the media. "I don't even understand rape, but I have lived all these years with that mark." And in a 2007 interview, "I was so sure that the truth would come out — that they knew it was not me — that I told my lawyer not to even tell me if they [prosecutors] offered a plea bargain."

But a Harris County jury — drawn from politically conservative registered voters who tend to favor conviction over acquittal — convicted Taylor in May 1995. The prosecutor's case was circumstantial: the victim made an in-court identification, and a serologist from the Houston Crime Lab testified that, since no semen had been found on the victim's sheet, Taylor could not be excluded as the assailant. The jury found Taylor guilty and assessed his punishment at sixty years in prison.

While the jury verdict devastated Taylor's family, his mother knew that the eldest of her five children was innocent, and she was not about to accept the verdict. She convinced the New York–based Innocence Project that her son was not guilty and secured their assistance in working toward his exoneration.

In 2006, the Innocence Project located the sheet. It had a wet spot. The Harris County District Attorney's Office cooperated with the Project's proposal to have an independent DNA test conducted on the sheet. Test results in the summer of 2007 revealed that Taylor was not the rapist. DNA from the wet spot on the sheet identified the assailant as Roosevelt Carroll, a longtime sex offender serving a sentence in the Texas prison system for failing to register as a sex offender.

Taylor's exoneration marked the third time that the mishandling of evidence by the Police Crime Lab in Houston had led to the wrongful conviction of a criminal defendant. In 2002 the local media conducted extensive investigations into the operations of the crime lab and exposed staggering negligence and mismanagement. These investigations in turn prompted city officials to conduct an audit of the lab's serology department. The audit resulted in the release of two inmates who had been wrongfully convicted of rape charges based on false and erroneous testimony of serologists from the crime lab. The exonerations prompted the closure of the crime lab's serology department.

In 2005, Mayor Bill White vowed to clean up the "disgraceful mess" associated with the crime lab and to restore integrity to its operations. The mayor assigned Michael Bromwich, a former U.S. Justice Department inspector, the task of investigating procedures at the crime lab and issuing recommendations. Bromwich completed his investigation in June 2007, identifying at least 180 cases in which the serology department had made major mistakes. Those cases are still awaiting prosecutorial and judicial review.

Taylor became the 201st person exonerated by DNA evidence in the United States. Former Harris County district attorney Charles Rosenthal promptly apologized to the wrongfully convicted man. "I feel awful," he said. "Nobody wants to have an innocent person wrongfully convicted and sent to prison."

Rosenthal vowed to apply as much pressure as possible to keep the actual rapist, Roosevelt Carroll, behind bars for as long possible. Scheduled for a 2010 good-time release, Carroll could be held until 2019. Rosenthal said that the serial sex offender would not receive any early release benefits. But Rosenthal couldn't prosecute Carroll for the rape because the five-year statute of limitations had expired.

Hidden in the postexoneration maneuvers in Taylor's case lies an official refusal to assign accountability for the wrongful conviction. The crime lab serologist who testified at Taylor's trial that no evidence of semen was found on the sheet worked at the lab between 1993 and 1998. In Taylor's case, the district attorney's office should have thoroughly investigated (1) whether the serologist even tested for semen and (2) if he did conduct those tests, what procedures he employed. Since Bromwich finished his review of the crime lab's serology department, no one has taken further official action in the 180 problem cases that he found.

The district attorney's office should conduct an in-house inquiry into the actions of the prosecutor who handled the Taylor case. The initial police report clearly stated that investigators observed a "wet spot" on the sheet on which the rape occurred. The prosecutor had access to that initial report and knew before the trial that the crime lab's serologist would testify that no "semen" had been found on the sheet. That lab finding should have triggered a red flag in the prosecutor's mind. The wet spot was there. The prosecutor should have examined the lab report thoroughly and questioned the serologist about his testing methodology.

Further, the victim did not pick Taylor out of a

physical lineup. She identified him in the presence of a lone police officer who brought her a videotape. At some point, while viewing this videotape, she suddenly remembered that her assailant had a missing tooth. We cannot know whether this recollection came after she viewed Taylor and saw his missing tooth. The prosecutor had an ethical responsibility to make sure that the victim's pretrial identification was not tainted in any way, particularly since there was no independent corroboration of her identification of Taylor as the assailant.

The district attorney's office and the Texas attorney general's office should ask the Texas legislature for uniform eyewitness identification procedures for all state law enforcement agencies. Texas should follow the lead of New Jersey and Minnesota in implementing such mandatory uniform procedures, which have built-in safeguards against mistaken identifications.

The conduct of Taylor's trial counsel also begs scrutiny. Taylor professed his innocence. His family staunchly supported his claim. The defense attorney should have secured an independent polygraph examination of his client. Polygraph results are inadmissible in a criminal trial, true, but they remain an excellent investigative lever that a defense attorney can use in pretrial negotiations with the prosecutor. Armed with a favorable polygraph finding, defense counsel might have been able to convince the prosecution that the extraordinary videotaped lineup procedure might have produced a mistaken identification.

Defense counsel should also have moved the court for independent testing of the wet spot on the sheet. He could have gained access to that initial police report identifying the wet spot with a timely Brady request. Defense counsel should have spoken to the investigating officers to determine if other sex offenses had occurred in that particular neighborhood, or if the police had identified any other sex offenders living in the area. Roosevelt Carroll lived less than a mile from the Taylor residence.

Finally, defense counsel should have contacted the neighbor who told police that she had seen Taylor in the vicinity prior to the rape. How did she know Taylor? What motivated her to give his name to the police as a possible suspect? Her statements provided the officers with probable cause to arrest Taylor, and it was flimsy probable cause, to say the least.

Attorney Shelton Sparks did not represent Taylor at trial but handled his appeal.

"We had concerns from the beginning that this was a case of mistaken identification," Sparks told the media following Taylor's exoneration. "But we did not pursue DNA testing, because we did not believe there was any evidence to be tested based on the [HPD analyst's] testimony at trial."

Hindsight is indeed 20/20. But plenty of evidence in the record should have prompted questions: the initial police report, the physical evidence on the sheet, and the serologist's testimony. Although the serologist said that no semen was found on the sheet, he did not say the sheet had been destroyed. The Innocence Project was able to locate the sheet in 2006 and have it tested, clearly recognizing the significance of the wet spot. Why didn't Taylor's trial counsel and appeal counsel recognize its significance as well?

Officials responsible for investigating, prosecuting, and defending Ronald Gene Taylor did not by any stretch of the imagination carry out their duties in a proper, adequate manner. It is admirable that the district attorney's office now wants to do everything it can to keep Roosevelt Carroll in prison, particularly since it cannot prosecute him for the rape for which Taylor was wrongfully convicted.

Texas will pay Taylor $50,000 for each year he was wrongfully imprisoned, but he may have other legal remedies. First, there is potential civil liability for the Houston crime lab because of its mishandling of the evidence. The crime lab would enjoy only qualified immunity for any deliberate mishandling or falsifying of evidence. While the district attorney and the victim are insulated with absolute immunity from civil liability in any wrongful conviction action, the nosey neighbor is subject to civil liability depending upon what she told police and in what context she provided damaging information against Taylor. And, finally, the police themselves could be subject to civil liability depending upon their conduct in the arrest and lineup procedures.

Cases like those of Ronald Gene Taylor and at least three dozen others involving DNA exonerations in Texas create a need for the state legislature to establish an innocence commission empowered to investigate all cases involving wrongfully convicted persons. Such a commission would serve the interests of the general public and the state's judicial system. As the matter now stands, taxpayers receive a $50,000-a-year bill for each wrongfully convicted person. Taxpayers should be informed about who was responsible for a wrongful conviction as well as why and how it occurred.

An innocence commission could make these determinations following a thorough investigation. The commission would report its findings to the Texas Legislature, providing public accountability for wrongful criminal convictions that not only damage the innocent and burden taxpayers but undermine the integrity of Texas's criminal justice system.

Not willing to wait for legislative action on the innocence commission issue, the Texas Court of Criminal Appeals in June 2008 took its own steps to address the increasing number of DNA exonerations in the state. The court established the Texas Criminal Justice Integrity Unit and charged it with the responsibility of investigating and correcting weaknesses in the state's criminal justice system.

"This is a call to action to address the growing concerns with our criminal justice system," wrote Court of Criminal Appeals judge Barbara Hervey. "Although we applaud all previous studies and dialogue, it is now time to act and move for reform."

The Integrity Unit was created after calls to the legislature by prominent state leaders to establish an innocence commission failed. Chief Justice Wallace Jefferson of the Texas Supreme Court and presiding judge Sharon Keller of the Court of Criminal Appeals were among those leading the appeal to the legislature to create an innocence commission. The need for such a commission gained legitimacy in May 2008 after nine exonerated men urged Texas lawmakers in Austin to address the causes for wrongful convictions but the lawmakers did not act.

"There has been a realization that we have to do something and we have to keep moving on it," Judge Hervey concluded.

Hervey said the Integrity Unit will work closely with Governor Rick Perry and State Senator Rodney Ellis, D-Houston, a longtime activist in innocence projects who was appointed to the unit. The Integrity Unit will seek guidance from various innocence projects and legal clinics to identify potential problems and implement corrective measures. Hervey said some of the critical issues that the Integrity Unit will address include but are not limited to the following: 1) the quality of legal representation for indigent criminal defendants; 2) improvements in witness identification procedures; 3) overhauling and creating new standards for the collection, preservation, and storage of evidence; and 4) creating a review process for cases of current inmates who may have been wrongfully convicted.

Senator Ellis praised the court for establishing the unit saying it was "showing some leadership. We know the problems, and we know some of the solutions. We can put a dent in the problem."

Dallas district attorney Craig Watkins was also appointed to the Integrity Unit. "They are on the right path in Austin," he said. "With seventeen exonerations in Dallas and thirty-three in Texas, we can't turn a blind eye to that."

Beyond its public apology, the only solution offered by the Harris County district attorney's office for the wrongful conviction of Ronald Gene Taylor was to guarantee greater punishment for the real rapist, Roosevelt Carroll. Exacting greater punishment from the real rapist is not the issue. The real issue is how to prevent the horrendous injustices done to the innocent like Ronald Gene Taylor. His case and others like it clearly show how easy it would be for Texas to execute an innocent man in a similar rush to judgment.

10

Child Rape

In June 2008, the U.S. Supreme Court struck down the death penalty for child rape in *Kennedy v. Louisiana*. The decision caught the attention of then presidential candidates John McCain and Barack Obama, who went on record as disagreeing with it.

"Today's Supreme Court ruling is an assault on law enforcement efforts to punish these heinous felons for the most despicable crime," McCain said.

"I think that the rape of a small child . . . is a heinous crime, and if a state makes a decision that under narrow, limited, well-defined circumstances, the death penalty is at least potentially applicable . . . that does not violate our Constitution," said Obama.

The statements of both men are troubling. McCain failed to mention murder when he called child rape *the* most despicable crime. And during his campaign, Obama frequently touted his efforts as a state senator to reform the Illinois death penalty system, presumably to attract voters opposed to capital punishment. But the statements by both men — which reflect the views of many Americans — casually asserted that child rape should rank alongside first-degree murder in deserving the death penalty.

The taking of a human life — by capital murder, second-degree murder, manslaughter, or negligent homicide — is a heinous crime. Whether the victim dies during an armed robbery, in a car accident caused by a drunk driver, or in a barroom fight, a life has been extinguished. Yes, raping a child is despicable, but killing someone is far worse.

More than three decades ago, the Supreme Court held that the death penalty for the rape of an adult woman was cruel and unusual punishment. Those who supported the death penalty for child rape tried to distinguish child rape from adult rape by arguing that the child's suffering is as horrific as the consequences of murder.

Obama's view — advocating the death penalty for child rapists under certain circumstances — opens a Pandora's box of legal questions that could paralyze the courts with countless appeals arguing about the degree of horror inflicted on a young rape victim. How can a society decide which child rape deserves the death penalty?

There are more than half a million registered sex offenders in this country, many of whom were convicted of child rape and many of whom were raped themselves as children. How many of them should have received the death penalty? When is the rape of a child just another rape, and when is it a death penalty rape? What if the victim is too young to talk or remember? If we can try children as adults, can they be raped as adults, too?

The reality, of course, is that sentencing would come down to the discretion of juries, as it does in murder cases. We could expect to see racial bias in these verdicts as we have seen in capital cases, particularly in the South, where blacks convicted of murder more frequently find themselves sentenced to death than other racial groups.

Taking these historical lessons into account, a black defendant charged with the rape of a white child would likely get the death penalty. Upper- and middle-class white offenders would likely benefit from plea bargains. There would inevitably be unjust, disparate sentencing: a black man who rapes his twelve-year-old daughter might get the maximum penalty while a white man who rapes his five-year-old daughter might get a probated sentence.

Does it make sound criminal justice policy to increase the number of possibly innocent men facing the death penalty by enacting laws authorizing that penalty for child rapists? The facts outlined by the Supreme Court in *Kennedy v. Louisiana* striking down the death penalty for child rapists in June 2008 illustrate this potential for wrongful convictions.

Patrick Kennedy was the first person to receive a death sentence under Louisiana's child-rape law. The eighth-grade dropout, who has an IQ of 70 and whose only criminal behavior consisted of issuing five worthless checks between 1987 and 1992, called 911 on March 2, 1998, to report the rape of his eight-year-old stepdaughter. Kennedy told the 911 operator that the girl had been in the garage when he heard her screaming. He rushed outside to find her in the yard adjacent to the house. The girl told him that two teenage boys who lived in the neighborhood had dragged her from the garage where she was selling Girl Scout cookies and raped her in the yard. Kennedy also told the operator that he saw one of the teenagers, who appeared to be about eighteen, riding away on a blue ten-speed bike.

When the police arrived at the scene, Kennedy escorted the officers into his daughter's bedroom, where they observed that she was bleeding vaginally. The young girl was rushed to the hospital and underwent emergency surgery. Then investigators interviewed her. She told them exactly what she had told the doctors: two teenage boys had raped her. In one three-hour interview with a social worker and a psychologist, she described exactly how the boys assaulted her before fleeing on bicycles.

Two days later, police recovered a blue bicycle hidden in tall grass behind a nearby apartment. The bike matched the description Kennedy had provided to the 911 operator, although it didn't have as many gears and its tires were flat. Nearby, police found a black shirt like the one the young girl said one of her assailants had been wearing. The bike and shirt belonged to a black teenager named Devon Oatis who matched the description the girl had given to investigators of one of her assailants.

The police, however, ruled Oatis out as a suspect. They noted that the abandoned bicycle didn't work and Oatis was "heavy set" while the victim described the assailant as "muscular."

Investigators then turned their attention to Kennedy, even though no direct evidence supported their suspicions. They had found blood on the underside of the victim's mattress, which led them to theorize that the rape had occurred in the child's bedroom and Kennedy had flipped the mattress to conceal the blood. When investigators spoke to a dispatcher at Kennedy's place of employment, the employee said Kennedy had called in saying he could not report to work that morning because his daughter had "become a lady." In the minds of the investigators, this statement bolstered their theory, so they pressed on. They spoke to a carpet cleaning service and learned that Kennedy had scheduled an emergency cleaning.

Yet even despite this mounting circumstantial evidence, the child's mother refused to believe her husband had molested her daughter.

Two weeks after the crime, police arrested Kennedy, and Child Protection Services removed the girl shortly thereafter from her mother's home, stating that "Mrs. Kennedy believes the story that her daughter tells her about two strangers dragging her from the garage and raping her on the side of their house." CPS workers said the child needed protection from her mother's "negative influences" and recommended treatment because of "allegations of sexual abuse by stepfather" and because the "mother is denying abuse" and because the child has alleged "other perpetrators [when] evidence points to stepfather." CPS officials informed the child's mother that she could regain custody of her daughter once she learned to be "objective concerning the evidence" and accept that Kennedy had raped the child.

The court record shows that at this point, the mother started telling her daughter that she believed Kennedy had raped her. She consoled the child by telling her that it would be okay if she told authorities that Kennedy had raped her. CPS then allowed the child to return to her mother. Some twenty months after the rape, investigators from CPS, the sheriff's department, and the district attorney's office interviewed the child, who said that Kennedy raped her early that morning, causing her to faint.

As in many states, Louisiana prosecutors need only the word of the victim to secure an aggravated rape indictment. Louisiana elected to charge Kennedy with a capital offense. The trial court rebuffed challenges by defense counsel to the capital indictment. When defense counsel finally gained access to the victim's mattress for independent forensic testing, those tests revealed that the blood on the mattress matched neither the blood type of the victim nor of Kennedy. The prosecution immediately moved for a continuance, informing the court that it needed more time to change its theory of the crime. The court granted the continuance.

Patrick Kennedy went on trial in August 2003. It was difficult to seat a jury. The trial court dismissed forty-four prospective jurors because they either opposed the death penalty on principle or could not impose it for aggravated rape. Once a jury was seated, the prosecution did not present any "positive evidence" that Kennedy committed the rape. Although it had performed forensic testing on the bloodstains on the mattress as well as medical testing on the victim, the prosecution said its forensic testing was "inconclusive." Then the prosecutor put the child on the witness stand. She quickly lost her composure and never described the rape to the jury.

Kennedy's defense counsel presented the theory that Oatis was the actual rapist. This theory supported the victim's initial and oft-repeated claims about being raped by two teenagers. Defense counsel, however, couldn't get Oatis into court because he had fled the state to avoid a subpoena. The jury found Kennedy guilty and, because the victim was under twelve years of age, recommended a death sentence.

The circumstantial nature of the evidence — particularly the lack of any corroborating physical evidence — in the Kennedy case is disturbing. But equally troubling is the lack of equity in one of the largest series of child rape cases in the United States.

While on Shepherd One, heading to America in April 2008, Pope Benedict XVI informed reporters that he was "deeply ashamed" of the sex abuse scandals that have rocked the Catholic Church in the United States for the past twenty-five years. He said the scandals caused him "great suffering." These scandals involved priests sexually abusing young children, mostly male. Many of these priests were convicted of a litany of sex-related offenses, including aggravated rape, and most of their victims were under the age of twelve.

"It is difficult for me to understand how it was possible that priests betray in this way their mission . . . to these children," the pope told reporters. "We are deeply ashamed, and will do whatever is possible so that this does not happen in the future. We will absolutely exclude pedophiles from the sacred ministry. It is more important to have good priests than many priests. We will do everything possible to heal this wound."

"Everything possible" in this case means throwing a great deal of money at the victims. In recent years, the dioceses of Boston, Charleston, Dallas, Los Angeles, Louisville, and Orange all reached multimillion-dollar payout settlements with sex abuse survivors. But even the Church's coffers have limits. The dioceses of Davenport,

Portland (Oregon), San Diego, Spokane, and Tucson all filed for bankruptcy either to avoid settlements or in addition to them. All told, the American arm of the Church has paid out some $2 billion in settlement costs since 1950.

The first major pedophile priest scandal broke in Louisiana in 1983 when police arrested Father Gilbert Gauthe for abusing hundreds of children, many of them altar boys. He was indicted in October 1984 for one count of aggravated rape of a minor less than twelve years of age, and eleven counts each of aggravated crime against nature, immoral acts with a minor, and contributing to the delinquency of a juvenile by taking pornographic pictures. Gauthe received a twenty-year sentence in 1985 through a plea bargain and served ten years in the state's prison system before being released through good-time.

All priests like Gauthe would have been eligible for the death penalty under the Louisiana child-rape law struck down by the Supreme Court. Four other states — Florida, Montana, Oklahoma, and South Carolina — had the death penalty for child rape on the books but had not used it in decades. Texas enacted a child-rape law during the state's 2007 legislative session that could be applied only to offenders with prior rape or sexual assault convictions. Significantly, six other states — Alabama, California, Pennsylvania, Tennessee, Utah, and Virginia — rejected efforts by lawmakers and victims' rights advocates to enact laws that would have instituted capital punishment for child rape.

States that sanction the death penalty for child rape stand in league with countries like Egypt, Jordan, Nigeria, Saudi Arabia, and the United Arab Emirates, which also impose the death penalty for rape. The last execution in America for rape was in 1964. Since 1930, a total of 455 people in America were executed for rape, 405 of whom were black men convicted almost exclusively of raping white women.

Despite these historical racial inequities in capital rape laws, New Orleans sex crimes prosecutor Kate Bartholomew sees no moral or legal problem with executing child rapists. "In my opinion," she told the media after oral arguments were heard in the Supreme Court in the Kennedy case, "the rape of a child is more heinous and hideous than a homicide. It takes away their innocence, it takes away their childhood, it mutilates their spirit, it kills their soul. They're never the same after these things happen."

Kennedy's appellate attorney Bill Sothern disagreed. "When we look at what it means to be cruel and unusual," he said in media interviews, "this is exactly the kind of thing that raises these serious concerns of the constitutionality of Mr. Kennedy's death sentence. When we look at the death penalty in the South, we always need to be conscious of the role that race plays. And I think that the fact that Mr. Kennedy [is] a black [man] from Jefferson Parish, a place with a troubling record of racial discrimination, I think that that speaks volumes."

But it was Judy Benitez, executive director of the Louisiana Foundation Against Sexual Assaults, who raised the most troubling question about the death penalty in child rape cases. She pointed out that wrongful prosecutions are higher in cases involving children because they are more susceptible to suggestive, leading questions by prosecutors.

The first DNA exoneration in this country occurred

in 1989 and involved a wrongful conviction in a rape case. By 1996, the U.S. Justice Department was reporting that at least 25 percent of all persons convicted in sex offense cases in this country were innocent and had been wrongly convicted. By 2007, studies revealed that 85 percent of those exonerated in sex offenses were black males convicted of raping white women.

A punishment highly influenced by traditional racism and cultural prejudice, the death penalty stains our nation's soul. Of the 1,135 persons executed from 1977 through November 30, 2008, 934 were put to death in southern states. Texas and Virginia alone executed 525 of those persons. It would take nearly nine years to kill the 3,309 inmates on the nation's death rows today as of January 1, 2008, if one inmate were executed each day. And since juries hand out approximately 120 new death sentences each year, two persons would have to be executed every third day to keep the nation's death rows empty.

It might take years, but it could be done. America could join ranks with China, which executed at least 470 people in 2007, making it the death penalty capital of the world, according to Amnesty International. Iran came in a close second with 377 executions, including the stoning of a man who committed adultery and the execution of a thirteen-year-old boy for an unknown offense. Amnesty International also reported that in 2007, from an estimated population of 27,500 on the world's death rows, some 3,347 executions took place in fifty-one countries. One of those executed was an Egyptian beheaded in Saudi Arabia for sorcery.

While outright abolition of the death penalty in the United States seems an impossible dream, hope still flickers. Public support for executions has declined over the last ten years, although as many as 65 percent of Americans still favor capital punishment for at least some murders. Some jurors who once voted for the death penalty are having second thoughts about their decisions. When in 2006 Kenneth Boyd became the thousandth person to be executed in North Carolina, two of the jurors who had voted for his death sentence pleaded with the governor to spare the killer's life.

Susan Childress, writing in *Newsweek* on October 27, 2007, pointed to the Louisiana case of Dan Bright, sentenced to death in 1996. The forewoman of the jury in the Bright case, Kathleen Hawk Norman, later filed an amicus brief in support of his effort to win a new trial. Bright's conviction was reversed in 2006, leading to his release from prison. Norman has since formed Jurors for Justice, an advocacy group for jurors haunted by the death verdicts they have imposed. *Newsweek* reported that before his release, while still in shackles, Bright told Norman: "You were used like I was used. Do me a favor — don't forget about the others."

11

The Killers of Women

Men who kill women frequently escape death themselves in the nation's execution chambers. Women, considered chattel — mere property — in the eyes of the law for centuries, were not afforded full equality in the United States until the twentieth century.

The first shelter for battered women did not appear until 1974 in St. Paul, Minnesota. Two decades later there were still more than twice as many animal shelters as shelters for abused women in the United States. Yet domestic abuse accounts for a shocking number of homicides in the United States each year. Between 1976 and 2005, 64,529 homicides took place as a result of domestic violence. In 2006, nearly 23 percent of all homicide victims were women.

Annual reports by the United States Justice Department consistently reveal that two-thirds of all incidents of violence against women involve a relative or someone they know. Six times as many women are victimized by their intimate partners as by strangers.

Violence involving an intimate partner is an epidemic. The Centers for Disease Control reported in 2003 that there were 5.3 million such victimizations, with 550,000 requiring hospital treatment. In 1995, 1,252 women were killed by intimate partners. In 2000, the number remained essentially the same: 1,247.

Men who kill their intimate female partners are almost never charged with first- or second-degree murder. They generally plea-bargain down to a lesser grade of homicide — manslaughter, for instance — and serve less time than drug dealers and car thieves. Men who kill their wives and lovers rarely receive the death penalty, regardless of how coldblooded or vicious their crimes may be. Several inmates I met during my four-decade incarceration became what I term "character studies" — examples of the strange, twisted mindset it takes to kill a woman and justify it as a prerogative conferred on men when they deem it to be the manly thing to do.

LEON HORNE

Leon Horne is one of these character studies. I worked with him in the prison laundry at the Wade Correctional Center between 1996 and 2003. He was a throwback to the "convict guards" who once ruled the Louisiana prison system with brute force. Prison officials made these inmates "guards," giving them permission to beat prisoners and inflict other punishments equally as brutal. A snitch by nature who frequently ratted out other inmates, Horne was more than qualified for such a job.

He arrived in the N5 Protection Unit at the David Wade prison in 1995. Because he had been a reserve deputy with the Ouachita Parish Sheriff's Department, he was assigned to the protection unit, which housed former prison guards, law enforcement officers, high-profile government witnesses, and juveniles tried as adults: anyone other prisoners might take advantage of or assault for revenge.

Horne was called Ace Boon Coon. In southern prison vernacular, the moniker meant "top nigger." The term didn't offend Horne; in fact, he embraced it. A prison guard called Shorty gave him the nickname. Horne was a dirty cop, the kind who believes that graft and corruption go hand in hand with law enforcement.

The Horne case began on a March morning in the early 1990s in Monroe, Louisiana. Horne was sitting in his car at a local Cracker Barrel store. He spoke briefly to a friend who passed the car. The friend later recalled that Horne seemed "unhappy about something."

That wasn't unusual. Horne always seemed angry and depressed. At age eight, he had watched his father shoot his mother in the face and then turn the gun on himself. The psychological scars from that trauma fostered a recurring depression. Horne used it to justify a life of failure: as a husband, a father, and a cop. It was his personal license to unleash explosive anger at anyone or anything. But when he in turn murdered his own wife, he couldn't follow the act with suicide as his father had done.

That fateful March morning, Horne sat in his idling car in front of Cracker Barrel, tapping the steering wheel fretfully. His stomach churned with anger, then bubbled into rage when he saw his wife's GMC van headed toward the store. Witnesses said Leon Horne's brown Dodge roared to life and exploded out of the store's parking lot, ramming directly into Patricia Horne's van.

The collision blew out one of the van's tires. Patricia Horne frantically maintained control of her vehicle, hitting the accelerator and desperately trying to speed away. The dislodged grille of the Dodge sparked and clanged on the pavement as Horne pulled alongside the passenger side of his wife's van. On a two-lane road, the speeding vehicles forced other motorists to swerve into neighborhood yards. Then Leon Horne fired two Ruger 9mm bullets into the side of the van.

Patricia Horne accelerated again, pulling ahead of the Dodge and attempting a right-hand turn in front of it. It was a fatal decision. Horne accelerated, ramming into the side of the van. This second collision pinned Patricia Horne's van against a guardrail on the driver's side of the car.

Cursing and consumed with rage, Leon Horne climbed out of his mangled Dodge and jumped on its hood. Patricia Horne was pleading for her life. Leon Horne leaned inside the van through the passenger window.

"Please, Leon, please don't—please, no," Patricia Horne screamed as she turned in a last desperate act to the driver's side window exposing the backside of her skirt, wet with urine.

Leon Horne pumped eleven 9mm bullets into her jerking, spasmodic body. Then he calmly got down off the hood of his car and walked away. Ignoring several passersby, he walked several blocks to his residence, the pistol at his side. Police quickly arrived at the scene of the shooting, where they recovered thirteen spent shell casings and a fully loaded 9mm clip. Patricia Horne lay dead in the driver's seat, her eyes fixed in a terrible stare.

The police then rushed to Horne's residence and surrounded it. He refused to come out.

"I can't go to jail," he screamed.

Several of Horne's law enforcement buddies arrived and tried to talk him into surrendering — a courtesy they would never have extended to any other criminal not holding hostages. After several hours of negotiations, Horne meekly surrendered.

At trial, Horne pled insanity. A psychiatrist testified that he "would likely respond with feelings of resentment and anger and at times violently when he feels slighted. He is a person likely to explode." Patricia Horne's decision to leave him was the "slight" Leon Horne used as an excuse to hunt her down and kill her.

Leon Horne's horrific crime merited the death penalty. He planned the murder. He put the Ruger 9mm in the Dodge with two thirteen-round clips — enough ammunition to commit a massacre. He drove to the Cracker Barrel and lay in wait for his wife. He rammed his vehicle into her van before running her down. And finally, while she begged for her life, he executed her with eleven 9mm bullets fired at point-blank range.

Although he committed a methodical, premeditated murder, the prosecution didn't seek the death penalty. Why? Patricia Horne was a victim of domestic violence. She was not a "crime victim." Domestic violence victims, almost all of them women, don't receive the societal benefit of death penalty justice when they are killed by spurned lovers and husbands. Since 1960, only two wife-killers have received the death penalty in Louisiana, and both killed multiple victims: their wives *and* their in-laws.

Only one of them was actually executed, perhaps because his wife was a cop.

Roy Fulghum

The first of these wife-killers with the death penalty was Roy Fulghum. He was on death row when I was there between 1967 and 1971. The *Furman* decision also spared him a trip to the electric chair.

In 1960, Fulghum had been married to Christine Massey for four years. They had two children, ages one and three. He was much older than his wife, which perhaps explained his jealousy. While the couple lived together at various times, they also lived from time to time with his wife's parents, William and Ruby Massey, in Shreveport. That living arrangement was a source of constant friction in the couple's marriage and gave rise to repeated arguments between Fulghum and his wife, and even more arguments between Fulghum and his mother-in-law. He had no problems with his father-in-law, or with his wife's younger brother, also named William, who was nineteen.

Friction in the Massey household became so frequent and frightening that Fulghum's wife and father-in-law had him placed under several peace bonds — today's equivalent of a restraining order — between March and May 1960. At one point, Fulghum was locked up in the local jail for several weeks before his wife withdrew most of those bonds. At his daughter's urging, William Massey secured Fulghum's release on June 2, 1960, even though he had asked that his son-in-law be kept under two peace bonds.

While Fulghum was jailed, a nearby tavern gave his wife a job. After his release, Fulghum moved in with the Masseys again. On June 15, an argument about Christine's job at the tavern erupted between Fulghum and Ruby Massey during an early dinner. Fulghum accused his wife of sleeping with tavern patrons. He packed his suitcase and stormed out of the Massey apartment at about 7:00 P.M.

He called a cousin, and the pair went to two different bars and chugged beer. Alcohol fanned the flames of his rage. He went to the residence of Wallace Smith, a friend, and borrowed a .22-caliber pistol, saying he wanted to do some frog hunting. He returned to one of the barrooms and wrote a note on the back of a guest check that read: "Would like for my kids to be left with my sister Mrs. J. R. Downing [address]. Tell Mrs. & Mr. Fulghum I'm sorry I had to do this but its the only way out. I love my wife and I will take her with me. Thanks to every one that stood by me. I love them with all my heart. I know I have did wrong to all. I hope to God will forgive me. Love Roy."

Fulghum then telephoned a sister, who also lived in Shreveport, and a brother who lived in nearby Keithville. He discussed the problems he had been having with his wife and his mother-in-law. His siblings counseled him to leave his wife and let the juvenile authorities resolve the custody issue with the children. He didn't take their advice.

Following the calls, Fulghum and his cousin took a cab back to the cousin's home. The cousin urged Fulghum to spend the night there, but Fulghum declined, saying he was going to get a room at a local motel near the Massey apartment. He then instructed the cab driver to take him to the motel. But he didn't go in. Instead he walked down the street.

He entered the Massey apartment, cursing and threatening his wife. Ruby Massey interrupted, defending her daughter. Without flinching, Fulghum turned and shot his mother-in-law twice, killing her instantly. The shot awoke the younger William Massey, who got up to investigate the commotion. Fulghum shot him twice; one of bullets pierced the young man's brain. Christine turned away in a frantic attempt to protect one of the children sleeping in a crib in the corner of the room. Fulghum turned and methodically shot her, killing her before she could even reach the child. She fell to the floor between the crib and the chair where her mother had fallen. The elder William Massey rushed into the room, and Fulghum shot him in the stomach and again in the back as he turned to run. Massey managed to escape from the house through a window in the next room but collapsed on the ground a short distance away. Fulghum's wife and mother-in-law had died instantly, but the two William Masseys didn't die until the following day at a local hospital.

Fulghum was tried, convicted, and sentenced to death for the four murders. He was released from the Louisiana State Penitentiary in 1984 on a medical furlough, having served twenty-four years for four coldblooded murders.

Leslie Lowenfield

Leslie Lowenfield was the other wife-killer who received the death sentence. The same year that Fulghum was released from prison, Lowenfield was sentenced to death in a Jefferson Parish courtroom after a jury convicted him of three counts of first-degree murder and two counts of manslaughter.

Lowenfield hailed from Guyana, on the northeast coast of South America. He arrived in New Orleans in June 1981. Two months later, Sheila Thomas, a Jefferson Parish sheriff's deputy, and her daughter moved in with Lowenfield. Their relationship was violent from the outset. On several occasions, Thomas left Lowenfield and returned to her mother's home. These separations created more tension, producing in Lowenfield a deep-seated bitterness.

After nine months of living with Lowenfield's abuse, Thomas left him for the last time and moved in with her mother. Lowenfield instigated a campaign of harassment against Thomas and her family, and he was especially bitter toward her mother, Myrtle, whom he blamed for the couple's estrangement. Thomas filed complaints against Lowenfield with the Jefferson Parish Sheriff's Department.

In June 1982, he was arrested for making obscene telephone calls to Thomas, attempting arson, and resisting arrest. But when Thomas withdrew her complaints, the charges were dismissed. This gesture of reconciliation failed to appease Lowenfield. He repeatedly told others that he was going to get Thomas and her family, telling one friend that he was going to "blow Sheila's fucking brains out." He told the friend that women in his country did not leave their men.

On August 29, 1982, Lowenfield saw Thomas's vehicle parked at another man's house. He went to the apartment of another friend and told her he was about to "kill Sheila." He also said he was going to kill Thomas's mother and the father of Thomas's four-year-old daughter. He was spinning out of control.

The following day, Owen Griffin, Thomas's stepfather, was sitting in a vacant lot near his home playing cards with neighbors. Shots rang out from his home. Griffin jumped up and rushed inside. More shots rang out. Neighbors quickly called the police, who arrived within minutes.

When police entered the Griffin residence, they found the bodies of Sheila Thomas, her daughter, her daughter's father, her mother, and her stepfather all sprawled on the living room floor. All the victims had been shot multiple times, and each had a bullet in the head. Police found a .38-caliber pistol and a .22-caliber semiautomatic rifle at the scene as well as a notebook containing Lowenfield's rants against Thomas and her family. The following excerpt reflects the hatred that consumed him:

> Your mother teach you all her bad ways . . . and now you have all her [w]horing ways. . . . I gave you all my money I had work[ed] for and now you want to play Big Shot, you [th]ink I do not know all you did to me But I [k]new your mother let you put [th]ings in my Food, and then you do not want to eat, you are not hungry, But Sheila, remember this, I got your hair your drass and more, I can hurt you at any time. So I will keep in touch with Friends just to hear about what you are saying and I can make you go to your grave So [don't] you push it I leave you still brea[th]ing and your baby So lets keep it that way . . . Be glad I did it this way You and Shantell and Carl and Ray still Breathing . . . You Fuck with

me and I will make you and Shantell go in the grave yard.

Five weeks after the murders, Lowenfield was arrested in New York City and sent to Rikers Island. While there, he wrote letters to his sister about the murders. They reflect the same rage expressed in the notebook found at the crime scene:

Everyone is looking that I killed 5 people But know one know But me and them and that is why God made me got all 5 of them without them getting me. All I will say [is] a mouse can be a killer when you ride him. . . . Know one will get Sheila if I could not get her. . . . I loves her and this [is] why I kill her. . . . Shantell get shot when Carl put her in front of him so he think I was playing when I said he and Sheila Fuck up my life. . . . If you keep in this world and people keep on like what these bitches Did to me in Louisiana I will have to kill more and more. Because I know I work for my money and then people played the Love game that they in love just to took me for what I got. . . . Just to let you all know when Sheila get shot and her mother got shot all the people they have done bad things too Sheila and her mother had to called all of them before they leave this earth. So they did not go easy. I had to help the bitch by sho[o]ting her twice to let her stop with the names in her last moments. . . . If he [one of Thomas's brothers] was not behind bars I would have stayed in that house and let him have his box too. But I knew he was JPCC [Jefferson Parish Correction Center], so I get whom I wanted the most and So I leave.

Less than four years after he was sentenced to death, the hate-filled Leslie Lowenfield was executed on April 14, 1988, in Louisiana's electric chair for the five murders. *Furman v. Georgia* saved Roy Fulghum, the other Louisiana wife-killer who also killed his in-laws. But there was no judicial "act of God" to prevent Lowenfield's execution. Not only did he kill five people, but one of his victims, his common-law wife, was a deputy sheriff. Jefferson Parish sheriff Harry Lee, the most powerful law enforcement officer in Louisiana, put Lowenfield on the fast track to the execution chamber. Throughout Lee's long reign as sheriff, every single defendant who killed one of his deputies met the same fate.

Leon Horne fared much better. He was a cop. He received a life sentence for the second-degree murder of his wife, and he quickly found official favor in Louisiana's prison system, where the killers of women enjoy special status in a hypermasculine world.

In fact, the Louisiana prison system routinely sends the killers of women to work in the governor's mansion. The highly coveted inmate assignment has two criteria: the prisoner must be black, and he must be serving a life sentence, usually for killing his wife or girlfriend.

Pepi LaBorde

Like Horne, Allen "Pepi" LaBorde killed a woman and escaped the death penalty. He was one of the correctional center's most influential inmates. He started out in the N5 Protection Unit because he was sixteen years old when he was convicted of killing a teenage girl who rebuffed his sexual advances and then throwing her body off a bridge into a local river.

LaBorde eventually worked his way out of the protective cellblock into general population at the prison, where his woodworking skills and his ability to operate heavy equipment made him an essential and trusted inmate. Like Horne, LaBorde joined inmate self-help groups and took part in all the institution's special projects programs. He used his skills and his position of privilege — along with a lot of state resources — to accumulate a substantial base of prison power. His privileged position allowed him to indulge in homosexual activities and operate a pornographic video business on the sly out of the prison's maintenance department.

Like Horne, Fulghum, and Lowenfield, LaBorde had an explosive temper, and he flew off the handle into uncontrollable fits of anger against staffers and inmates.

Shortly after Venetia Michael became the state's first female warden to oversee an adult male prison in 2002, LaBorde erupted in one of his classic rages. He picked up a hammer and struck a prison supervisor in the head. Then he stole the supervisor's truck and drove off the prison compound.

Despite his nasty temper, he was just about to be transferred to the State Police Barracks in Baton Rouge, a minimum custody facility in the heart of the capital. It was the most coveted inmate job assignment in Louisiana. The barracks had no guns, no bars, and no razor wire. Its gates opened directly onto Baton Rouge streets. Prisoners enjoyed a range of privileges that approximated life in the free world. All had essential jobs at the barracks or on the grounds of the state capitol.

During the high-speed chase that followed La-

Borde's hammer assault on the guard, his stolen pickup hit the car of a female guard on her way to work at Wade. She was seriously injured. LaBorde jumped out of the prison truck and fled a short distance into nearby woods, where he collapsed.

Faced with certain capture, he slit his wrists with a stray piece of glass and bled to death. At the time of his death, he had $25,000 dollars in his prison account from craft items he sold to visitors at the prison's twice-yearly "art festivals" and to prison officials and other admirers of his woodworking skills.

Under Warden Michael's direction, the prison went into official mourning. She also directed top-ranking prison officials to conduct meetings with inmate leaders to explain LaBorde's demise.

These inmate leaders — with whom LaBorde shared his pornography and ill-gotten gains — requested, and Warden Michael approved, a memorial service for the escaped killer. Members of Warden Michael's staff attended the service and expressed official condolences over the untimely death of a killer who murdered a teenage girl because she refused to have sex with him. The only thing that Warden Venetia Michael's administration didn't do in LaBorde's honor was lower the prison's flag to half-staff.

SAME CRIME, DIFFERENT PENALTY

Donald Benjamin murdered a woman he had never seen before in a vicious, virtually inexplicable rage. In 1965 he walked into a New Orleans laundromat where a young white couple was washing clothes. Armed with a large knife, Benjamin cut off the young woman's clothes, leaving her clad only in her panties. Her boyfriend tried to protect her, but the heavy-set black man attacked him, wounding him critically in the process. The young girl broke away and ran outside, where Benjamin caught up with her. He stabbed her so many times, the knife broke. She died a horrible death in the gutter where Benjamin left her.

Donald Benjamin received the death sentence, a common occurrence in black-on-white crime in Louisiana. *Furman v. Georgia* saved him from execution. Despite the life sentence he received when the U.S. Supreme Court set aside his death sentence, Benjamin was paroled in 1990 after serving twenty-five years for the brutal murder.

Between 1992 and 1999, the Louisiana parole board released seventy-one murderers. The average amount of time served by murderers who killed women was just twelve years. Among the inmates paroled after murdering women were a contract killer, a double murderer, and a sledgehammer killer.

The contract killer, David Albert, murdered his employer's wife with a bullet to the head. He served twenty years.

The double murderer, Paul "Tex" Chandler, killed his estranged girlfriend and her companion and wounded two other people when he walked into a Shreveport bar and opened fire during a drunken, emotional rampage. He served twenty-four years.

The sledgehammer killer, Dr. Louis Graham, murdered his sleeping wife and tried to blame it on an intruder, just as Captain Jeffrey MacDonald had in 1970. Graham served twelve years.

Like Horne, LaBorde, and Fulghum, Chandler and Graham showed themselves to be twisted and cowardly as they vented their uncontrollable anger on defenseless victims: women who loved them or inadvertently encountered them. Lowenfield was no different.

So why did Benjamin, Fulghum, and Lowenfield receive the death sentence while Horne, LaBorde, Graham, Albert, and Chandler did not?

Benjamin, black, received the death penalty because he killed a white woman during a rape attempt; Fulghum, white, received the death penalty because he killed four people. Lowenfield, a black, received the death penalty because he killed a law enforcement officer, who happened to be his common-law wife, and four others. Benjamin's social status and race resulted in his death sentence, while it was the sheer number of victims in the Fulghum and Lowenfield cases that resulted in theirs.

The women in the Horne, LaBorde, Graham, Chandler and cases were wives or girlfriends, making them victims of domestic violence, as opposed to crime victims, even though their killers murdered them in the same methodical, cold-blooded way as Benjamin, Fulghum, and Lowenfield murdered their victims.

David Albert, the black contract killer hired by a white farmer to kill the farmer's wife, didn't receive the death penalty. In that unusual case, Albert avoided death row by cooperating with authorities to convict the farmer who hired him.

Race and victim status still largely determine when the death penalty in America is imposed. And gender still confers special status on white men, as victims or perpetrators, which late-twentieth-century laws in Louisiana and elsewhere in the United States clearly reflect.

In *Law, Gender, and Injustice*, Joan Hoff wrote about the blatant discrimination against women until the latter years of the twentieth century:

> In 1970, for example, the Ohio Supreme Court held that a wife was "at most a superior servant to her husband . . . only chattel with no personality, no property, and no legally recognized feelings or rights." The 1974 Georgia legislature approved a statute that defined the husband as "head of the family" with the "wife . . . subject to him; her legal existence . . . merged in the husband, except as so far as the law recognizes her separately, either for her own protection, her own benefit, or for the preservation of the public order." Until the early 1980s, a Louisiana statute gave husbands exclusive control over the disposition of jointly owned community property.

Today, federal laws protect women from discrimination in the workplace. Perhaps it's time for statutes to protect them from discrimination in courtrooms as well, according them the same rights — and therefore the same consideration — given to victims who are male.

Killings in domestic violence cases are murder, plain and simple. If there is to be a death penalty, it should be applied equally to all who kill in cold blood.

12

The Crime Victims Movement

Newton Anderson died by lethal injection in Texas on February 22, 2007, for a double murder he committed eight years earlier. "For all those that want this to happen," he said in a final statement, "I hope you get what you want and it makes you feel better and gives you some kind of relief."

Did the mourners get what they wanted? Or were they left with an empty feeling?

After a murderer is executed, crime victims have no one to hate. The desire for revenge obscures what they may feel after an execution — after the killer's body goes to a funeral home or a pauper's grave, after the news stories about the impending execution stop and death protesters move on to the next case. What does the victims' rights movement say about that void?

It began in California in the late 1970s. Its first target of note was Willie Archie Fain, who in the 1960s killed a seventeen-year-old boy, then raped his teenage girlfriend. Relatives and friends of Fain's victims formed a Keep Fain In committee to stop his parole. The committee collected some 84,000 letters opposing his release. The victims' rights movement sprang to life from the committee's successful efforts to keep the convicted murderer in prison, public outrage against crime in general, and a growing dissatisfaction with the way the criminal justice system was functioning.

The survivors of the victims of crime have become known in our society as "crime victims," who make eloquent arguments for justice. Crushing loss strikes them suddenly, shattering their lives and dreams, introducing them to the ugly specter of violent death, filling them with grief and agony. Hate becomes their natural companion. The experience threatens to destroy their faith in God and humanity. Often, the emotional and psychological damage is irreparable.

I came to know this from the parents of J. C. Bodden. He was the thirty-year-old convenience store manager I shot during a robbery attempt in Baton Rouge on December 5, 1965. I had no intent to kill him. The bullet I fired was a wild shot in the dark as he chased me across the parking lot.

Later that night, I knelt, head down, in a muddy field where I had hidden my car from the police chasing me, and the word "killer" reverberated in my head. I would never again be an ordinary man. I had become Cain. Guilt made it hard to breathe.

I wrote letters to his family over the years expressing my remorse. I never received an answer. I wrote no more after C. Paul Phelps, the secretary of Louisiana's Department of Corrections, told me that my victim's family didn't ever want to hear from me again and they had asked him to make certain my letters would stop.

In 1990, twenty-five years after my crime, I finally saw my victim's father. He was being interviewed on television after a pardon board hearing in my case. "He kilt my boy," Harvey Bodden said in a quavering voice from his wheelchair. "My boy was a good boy." He must have been in his eighties by then, but his grief was fresh and raw. A quarter of a century had not erased it. I understood then that I had multiple victims. With one bullet fired in haste and fear, I had destroyed an entire family.

The anger experienced by the victims of violent crime begs release. Stifled, it becomes a cancer that eats away at heart and soul with hate and resentment. Expressed, it seeks ancient and absolute justice: an eye for an eye. Nothing but death for the offender will appease it. It demands the ultimate punishment. When the perpetrators of violent crimes do not receive the death penalty, crime victims demand "natural life," a sentence with no right to parole.

While organized anger has a legitimate role in the grieving process and in the nation's criminal justice system, it does not give the survivors of victims of violent crime the all-encompassing right to use the system to exact personal vendettas. The justice system cannot administer punishment equitably and reasonably when it responds exclusively to demands for vengeance. It must balance crime victims' needs, the collective interest of society to exact retribution, and the offender's prospect of rehabilitation.

The law is man's social savior. It protects him from

his worst enemy: himself. If the justice system permits revenge to dominate its decision-making process, then lynch law takes hold. No one can reasonably dispute that it is the justice system's obligation to respond to the collective interests of society's law-abiding majority. But that obligation should not impale the interests of the individual on the stake of vengeance.

Punishment for punishment's sake — without purpose or design — offends the basic judicial tenets of equity and fairness. Justice requires an even hand. It must respond to the demands of society while it weighs the facts in each case, continuously grappling with the gnawing question, How much is enough?

The family of my crime victim said that the death penalty was the only punishment that fit my crime. But the Supreme Court lifted my death sentence in 1972 along with the death sentences of all other inmates in the country. Louisiana then gave me a life sentence. It held the reasonable expectation that I would one day be a free man if I satisfied the criteria traditionally used in the state for measuring punishment and rehabilitation. The family of my crime victim said I was shown mercy enough when I was spared an appointment with the executioner. For close to four decades they adamantly opposed my release, foiling it again and again with letters, petitions, and the support of elected officials in the Louisiana House and Senate.

But a life sentence without parole is not mercy. It is a slower form of execution. Lifers suffer perpetual torment. They suffer each day simply for the sake of suffering, simply to appease revenge. Natural life surpasses death in its cruelty. Those who demand that unending punishment are either ignorant of its effect on inmates or they have lost all capacity for mercy.

When a loved one is killed, the survivors can bury the body but not the sorrow. Every morning for days, months, and even years, they awaken to their loss. Birthdays, anniversaries, and holidays become times to grieve, not to celebrate.

Dr. Elliot Luby, an expert on victimology, once said that "when your parent dies, you have lost your past. When your child dies, you have lost your future."

A wide circle of friends and relatives assembles to comfort and assist the parents of a murdered child, but that circle cannot know the parents' pain.

In her excellent book *The Courage to Grieve*, Judy Tatelbaum wrote:

> Confronting death is hard for us survivors. One of the consequences of the denial of death in our society is that we are often unskilled in coping with loss, be it our own or another's. We may want to help, but we don't know how. Having no idea what to do when we hear of death, many of us run away from helping the bereaved. However, there are many ways we can help.
>
> Our friendships and support are essential for our grieving friend to go through and complete the mourning process. We need to reach out and take the initiative. Our presence is the most valuable thing we can give. Our presence is far more important than our knowledge or our advice, for the companionship of family and friends is the greatest source of support and solace. We can help our grieving friend the most by sitting near, holding a

hand, giving a hug, passing a tissue, crying together, listening, sharing our feelings. In coping with loss the bereaved are greatly depleted of energy. The presence of others helps to renew them.

I learned these lessons from two crime victims who shared their pain and grief with me, honestly and sincerely without anger at my crime. In 1984 I met Vernon and Elizabeth Harvey. These two leading Louisiana crime victims advocates taught me a great deal about crime victims and the crime victims movement. I am grateful for the respect they accorded me as they shared their most private and sensitive memories of their murdered daughter.

Robert Lee Willie brutally murdered the Harveys' daughter, Faith Hathaway, four years before we met. Willie was on Angola's death row. As coeditor of the *Angolite*, the prison's inmate newsmagazine, I was allowed to attend a pardon board hearing at which Sister Helen Prejean and others sought clemency for Willie, and I interviewed Vernon Harvey after that hearing.

What I learned at the hearing about Faith Hathaway grieved me deeply. What I learned about the killer's cruelty troubles me to this day. On May 28, 1980, Faith Hathaway was to be inducted into the United States Army. Fluent in Spanish, French, and Creole, the eighteen-year-old girl planned to study Russian and perhaps become an interpreter. Faith loved to read about foreign places. Sometimes she read eight hours a day, dreaming of cities and countries she hoped to visit, longing for the adventures and joys of such a life. Tomorrow stood before her like a prophecy of happiness. Her parents instilled in her the belief that dreams were attainable with hope and effort.

On the night of May 27, she went out with friends to celebrate her last night as a civilian. They wanted to enjoy one last night of freedom before joining the disciplined, regimented life of military service. Faith went to the Lake Theatre Disco, a lounge in Mandeville, Louisiana. The night slipped into morning, and at approximately 4:30 A.M., Faith was standing in front of the disco when Robert Lee Willie and Joseph Vaccaro offered her a ride home. Sensing no danger, she accepted.

But Willie and Vaccaro didn't take Faith to her home in St. Tammany Parish. Instead, they took her to Fricke's Caves, a secluded and heavily wooded area in Washington Parish. They repeatedly raped and tortured her before they stabbed her to death. No one except the killers knows everything that happened that night. We do know that after raping her Willie or Vaccaro or both held her hands while one of them stabbed her repeatedly in the throat.

"Go away, and let me die by myself," she begged her killers.

After their sadistic sexual frenzy, Faith's body was almost unrecognizable.

The Harveys had to wait two agonizing days before their daughter's purse and clothes turned up. During that nightmare of uncertainty, desperate prayers fell silently from their lips. Even after Faith's belongings were found, they hoped that she would be found alive. They couldn't understand why such tragedy had befallen them.

On June 4, the Harveys learned the bitter truth. Faith's battered, mutilated body had been discovered where the killers left it. Still, her parents clung to hope. They wanted to be sure the body was actually their daughter. Elizabeth Harvey asked her brother, a dentist, to make a positive identification using Faith's dental records.

"I never realized then what a hard thing I asked my brother to do," Elizabeth Harvey told me.

Vernon Harvey and his wife began to live with daily grief, as I'm sure the parents of my victim did. Grief, they said, has no timetable. It affects each parent differently. They learned — among many painful, searing lessons — that it can cause marital friction. Some crime victim experts say that as many as 90 percent of parents whose children have been murdered experience serious marital difficulty within months of the death.

Stanley Ott, bishop of the Roman Catholic Diocese of Baton Rouge, said in a 1984 interview with the *Angolite* that he believed bereaved parents should have strong religious guidance as they work through their grief.

> From a human point of view, I would understand the anger and outrage, the very strong emotional feelings parents experience when their child is taken in such a violent way. I would be understanding of these natural feelings and try to assist them in coping with the feeling.
>
> But as a religious leader, I would pray with them asking that God guide and direct us. Many times when we come across the mysteries of life, like the unexplained loss of a loved one by a criminal act, we expect immediate answers to some hard questions. We should compose ourselves in prayer, and while faith will not take away the pain of our

loss, I believe that prayer, in God's spirit, will help us to understand and live with our grief. God is the Good Shepherd. He is going to be their support and help. Their pain will be eased through his mercy.

In 2000, Pope John Paul II visited Italy's horribly overcrowded prisons.

Afterward, the pope urged the government "in the name of Jesus for a sign of clemency toward all prisoners."

"Prisons," he warned, "cannot be used as a means of social retaliation or institutionalized vendettas. Punishment and prison make sense only if, while affirming the needs of justice and discouraging crime, they serve man's renewal. Prison must offer inmates the possibility to reflect and change their lives, in order to fully become part of civil society."

The Harveys taught me that there is no grief as powerful as that of a parent whose child has been murdered. As kind as they were to me, they burned with rage and hatred for their daughter's killer. Her death left a vacuum in their lives that they filled with the lust for revenge. Never had they been in the grip of such powerful emotions. They demanded that Robert Lee Willie be sentenced to death and they demanded the right to witness his execution.

"When they take him out of the chair," Vernon Harvey said, "I want to be there to see the smoke fly off his body."

Murder produces a bitter harvest that feeds the hunger for vengeance. I witnessed its grip on the Harveys. I began to understand what it must have done to my victim's family. So intense was Vernon Harvey's need for revenge that he read everything he could about crime and the death penalty.

"I actually rejoice when I find out someone has been executed," he said. "If I don't stay up at night to hear that they did it, it's the first thing I want to know in the morning."

Harvey's overriding need for revenge began as he sat through the trial of his daughter's killer and listened to the graphic details of how she was mutilated and tortured — a trial at which Willie mocked and taunted him. The scene was immortalized in Sister Helen Prejean's book *Dead Man Walking*.

"There was a time when I kept these feelings inside of me," Harvey said, "and I often wondered if I was going crazy for feeling as I do. But I've come to realize that other people not only understand but share my feelings as well. They want to see justice done. Justice will be done when they execute Robert Lee Willie and the rest of those people on death row."

The Harveys watched Robert Lee Willie die in Louisiana's electric chair on December 28, 1984. Prison officials didn't allow me to witness the execution, but I interviewed Harvey again some months after Willie's death. He told me then that he would witness the execution again and again if he could and that he would take pleasure in it each time. Willie's death seemed to have given him little peace.

Not all families of murder victims want offenders executed. In the May 29, 1998, issue of the *Houston Chronicle*, Celeste Dixon wrote about the murder of her mother and the futility of revenge:

When everyone around me was talking about the murderer in derogatory terms, using expressions like, "He'll get what's coming to him," or "We'll make him pay for what he did," my aching, broken heart could not help but respond. Since all I really wanted was for the pain to go away, I naturally assumed that what they were doing and saying was right, that a death sentence and execution would help take that pain away.

Later, I came to realize that those statements weren't taking my pain away. Instead, they were feeding my anger and hatred, which seemed to intensify the unbearable pain in my heart. The more I concentrated on my hatred for the murderer, the more I missed my mother and the angrier I got over losing her. I looked forward to the beginning of the trial and the promise of the death sentence which would bring an end to the pain for me and my family.

But a strange thing happened at the offender's trial. She began to see the murderer as a human being, not the monster the prosecution had made him out to be. She wrote:

Through my experience, I have come to believe that the greatest disservice you can do to victims' family members is to expect them to want the murderer to die. This is a tremendous burden to carry because it forces us to keep our anger alive and put our compassion aside, when for our own sakes we need to do the opposite.

I eventually reached a point where I could let go of my desire for the murderer to die, and then actually forgive him for what he did. It was those two things that finally helped me heal and get relief from the pain and to let go of the anger and hatred that is necessary to support capital punishment.

The election of President Ronald Reagan in 1980 and the law-and-order agenda he presented to the nation created fertile soil across the country for the demands of crime victims to grow. The movement quickly spread from California, where the cases of Willie Archie Fain and Gregory Powell, the onion field killer made famous by Joseph Wambaugh, had created it. The Reagan agenda — and in particular the rigidly conservative judges he appointed — accelerated the pace of executions nationwide and created a social climate receptive to the demands for revenge made by crime victims.

Then the media discovered the crime victims movement. When TV news directors and newspaper editors across the nation realized that crime stories increased circulation and ratings, a media war broke out. Crime grabbed more headlines and airtime than ever before. It has remained a staple of local newscasts ever since. As Joel Dyer said in his 2000 book *The Perpetual Prisoner Machine: How America Profits From Crime*, "In the 1980s, when the media corporations decided to dramatically increase their use of violent, crime-oriented content as a means of increasing ratings or pickup rates and thereby enhancing profits, it created a by-product — an exaggerated apprehension of crime throughout the general population." This conclusion by Dyer was based on U.S. Justice Department statistics that showed crime in America had been decreasing.

The unfortunate fact that the nation produced some

of its worst serial killers — John Wayne Gacy, Henry Lee Lucas, and Ted Bundy, to name only three — during this period only fueled what Dyer called the media's "violent, crime-oriented content." The crimes of these killers, and the media coverage of them, generated so much social outrage that they legitimized crime victims' demand for revenge. John Walsh — the bereaved father of six-year-old Adam Walsh, who disappeared in July 1981, probably murdered by Lucas and a cohort named Ottis Toole — became the spokesperson for the national crime victims movement. The public outcry for revenge articulated by Walsh and others silenced the interests of justice and the voices of reason.

As Walsh's popular *America's Most Wanted* and *Crime Stoppers* programs flourished, local news programs shifted from reporting crime to preventing crime. Law-and-order politicians jumped on the bandwagon. These conservative politicians became the real power in the legislative process. They passed a slew of "get tough on crime" laws that prompted an explosive growth in the nation's prison systems as states and the federal government sought to keep up with demands for more penitentiaries.

Then President Bill Clinton, a southerner, co-opted the law-and-order movement from the Republicans, shifting the movement to liberals and civil libertarians. Clinton gave the rigorous pursuit of law and order a political prominence that crossed gender, racial, and political lines. Support for the death penalty reached all-time highs during his administration. Prisons became more brutal and violent as penal administrators embraced the vengeful social climate. It became their quasi-official license to abuse, torture, and murder inmates. The federal judiciary created by Ronald Reagan blessed these actions by resurrecting the historical hands-off doctrine to keep inmates from filing lawsuits against abuse and torture.

In 1992, Richard Stalder became head of the Louisiana prison system. He promptly supported parole eligibility for lifers after twenty years. The public backlash, especially the outrage from crime victims' advocates, was so intense that he quickly abandoned the proposal. That political experience caused Stalder to abandon any notion of penal reform, and he established a repressive prison regime in Louisiana.

In 1996, Murphy "Mike" Foster, grandson of one of Louisiana's most racist governors, became governor of the state with the support of former Ku Klux Klan leader David Duke. Prominent crime victims' advocates who called themselves crime fighters supported Foster's candidacy. He rewarded Irvin Magri, a former New Orleans cop, and Peggy Landry, a New Orleans housewife who liked to be called Pistol-Packin' Peggy, with appointments to the state's pardon and parole boards. Foster also reappointed Stalder. The Department of Corrections secretary created a crime victims section within the DOC, emphasizing victims' rights over inmates' rights. Prisoners and those who supported prison reform fell on hard times. For eight years, pardons and paroles dwindled.

The same year that Foster became governor of Louisiana, promising a law-and-order-friendly administration, President Clinton signed into law the Antiterrorism and Effective Death Penalty Act (AEDPA) and the Prisoner Litigation Reform Act (PLRA). The first of these effectively eliminated the writ of habeas corpus for state prisoners, and the second slammed shut the doors of federal, and ultimately state, courts on prisoner abuse claims. Just as penal administrators abused the PLRA to keep prisoner abuse, torture, and murder hidden behind prison walls, the AEDPA became a license for state prosecutors to manufacture false evidence, suppress favorable evidence, and use perjured testimony to secure capital convictions that led to a steady stream of condemned inmates into the nation's death chambers.

America now executes serial killers and the mentally ill with the same gusto. We incarcerate children in adult prisons. More than 2 million prisoners languish in federal, state, and local prisons. We have more people behind bars on a per capita basis than any other country in the world.

The crime victims movement has hijacked the nation's criminal justice system. It no longer accommodates normal moral outrage or legitimate organized anger. It responds almost without question to all-consuming demands for revenge. Victims witness executions and say that's not enough.

Where do we go from here?

13

Youth Violence

In 2007 a seventeen-year-old in Atlanta shot and killed his mother and younger siblings, including a four-year-old sister, for no apparent reason. In a small town in East Texas that same year, a sixteen-year-old helped her seventeen-year-old boyfriend and two friends murder her mother and her two younger brothers. After the shootings, her father, suffering from multiple bullet wounds, managed to crawl out of the family home, which the teens had set on fire, to alert authorities. In March 2007, a seventeen-year-old boy beat a pregnant woman to death in Houston with a baseball bat one afternoon in a busy park after a minor traffic altercation.

Two of the worst murders in Houston history occurred in the half hour before midnight in a city park on June 24, 1993. The killers were kids, and their crimes were savage. Americans have done little, before or since, to prevent the conditions that bred these juvenile monsters. It is no longer legal to execute them. And no punishment seems to fit their crimes — or deter them.

In 1993, two girls, fourteen and sixteen, stumbled upon a gang initiation as they walked home from a party. The killers belonged to a teen gang, the Black and Whites. Led by eighteen-year-old Jose "Joe" Ernesto Medellin, the gang severely beat seventeen-year-old Raul Villareal and then drank beer to celebrate his acceptance into the gang. Derrick Sean O'Brien, Peter Cantu, Efrain Perez, and Roman Sandoval rounded out the group. Vernancio Medellin and Frank Sandoval, younger brothers of two gang members, also accompanied them.

Their victims, fourteen-year-old Jennifer Ertman and sixteen-year-old Elizabeth Pena, had spent the evening at a nearby apartment complex lounging by the swimming pool with a friend who lived there. As their 11:30 P.M. curfew approached, Ertman and Pena debated the quickest way to return to Pena's house. They decided to take a shortcut, which led down railroad tracks and through a city park where the gang was partying. The gang attacked the girls as soon as they saw them.

Medellin grabbed Elizabeth Pena and dragged her off the tracks, down an embankment into the park. When she tried to break his grip, he threw her to the ground. Pena cried out for help to Jennifer Ertman, who had managed to get away but then returned.

The gang raped both girls repeatedly. Medellin later bragged that he had "opened" one of them — that is, took her virginity — and that, after one of the other gang members finished raping her, he sodomized her.

After the brutal sexual assaults, the gang taunted the girls, telling them they were about to die. Medellin removed his shoelaces and strangled Pena with them. He and O'Brien used a red nylon belt to strangle Ertman, pulling it so tight that it snapped in two.

Then the gang stomped on their lifeless bodies. Authorities found the corpses four days later in Harris County's 90-degree heat. Ertman's body had three broken ribs. Several of Pena's teeth were missing. Gang members boasted so openly about the murders that the brother of one tipped off police. Officers took the entire gang into custody five days after the grisly killings.

O'Brien smiled broadly at news cameras after his arrest in the sensational case. He admitted to officers that he and other gang members had raped both girls and that he and Medellin had strangled Ertman. He had previously been arrested for shoplifting, assault, and stealing a van. During O'Brien's trial, a police officer testified that he had seen O'Brien and Cantu punch, kick, and drag a man across the floor at a fast food restaurant three months before the murders. One of O'Brien's crime partners testified that the two had stolen dozens of cars. He also said O'Brien and Cantu started fights with victims at random and frequently assaulted them to steal their shoes.

O'Brien was also a suspect in the murder of another woman. Patricia Lopez was found stabbed to death in another Houston park on January 4, 1993. In his testimony against O'Brien, Jose Medellin told the court that Cantu said he and O'Brien had killed Lopez. O'Brien didn't deny the killing. Police placed him at the scene of the crime when they found his fingerprints on beer bottles they recovered there.

O'Brien was convicted of capital murder in 1994 and sent to death row. Medellin and Cantu were also sentenced to death after their trials. Villareal and Perez received death sentences that were commuted to life following a Supreme Court decision in June 2005 that held that juveniles who were seventeen or younger when they committed their crimes could not be executed. Vernancio Medellin, who was fourteen at the time, was convicted of aggravated sexual assault and sentenced to forty years in prison.

In 2005, twelve years after the horrific murders, a comment from O'Brien appeared on an anti-death-penalty Web site: "I wonder how many children could be saved or kept living, who would otherwise die, with the monies states use to kill men and women on death row. . . . We bear the responsibility of showing our children how to be human, and if we can't our world will continue to suffer for it. Life is a miracle and therefore precious. Each time one is taken before its time, the world loses something special."

On July 11, 2006, at the age of thirty-one, Derrick Sean O'Brien paid the ultimate price for murders he had committed as a teen. "I am sorry," he said from the gurney in the Texas death chamber. "I have always been sorry. It is the worst mistake that I ever made in my whole life."

O'Brien was pronounced dead at 6:19 P.M., minutes after lethal chemicals flowed into his veins. Medellin was executed on August 5, 2008, while Cantu awaits the same fate on death row.

Little more than a decade before the Black and Whites rampage, the nation's big cities were dealing with a tidal wave of crime. *Time* magazine reported on the alarming trend in a cover story on violent crime on March 23, 1981, quoting then Houston police chief B. K. Johnson:

"We have allowed ourselves to degenerate to the point where we're living like animals. We live behind burglar bars and throw a collection of door locks at night and set an alarm and lay down with a loaded shotgun beside the bed and then try to get some rest."

Who, *Time* asked, was forcing Americans to live like frightened animals? Atlanta police chief George Napper had an answer. "There are a lot of young guys who just don't care, who go out and blow people away just for the hell of it."

Chief Daryl Gates of the Los Angeles Police Department concurred. "We've lost a whole generation. Totally lost. No self-discipline. Total indulgence. Drugs. Lack of respect for the law. Lack of respect for values. A whole generation thumbed its nose at everything that was held sacred in this country. America has to take a look at its heart and its soul."

At the same time, former Louisiana Department of Corrections secretary C. Paul Phelps told the *Angolite* that "the most dangerous creature in the world is the sixteen- or seventeen-year-old kid who comes from the ghetto. It makes no difference whether he's white, black, Hispanic, or Chinese."

In 1980, there were 1,814 murders in New York City, a new record, according to *Time*. That same year, cities like Los Angeles and Miami also experienced dramatic increases in all categories of violent crime — murder, rape, robbery, and aggravated assault. The *Time* article noted "something new about the way that Americans are killing, robbing, raping and assaulting one another. The curse of violent crime is rampant not just in the ghettos of depressed cities, where it has always been a malignant force to contend with, but everywhere in urban areas, in suburbs and peaceful countrysides. More significant, the crimes are becoming more brutal, more irrational, more random — and therefore all the more frightening."

The crimes of young murderers — kids who belong on soccer fields, basketball courts, and baseball fields — are possibly the most terrifying. And they have been increasing since the 1970s. In 2007, the Centers for Disease Control reported that youth violence is even more widespread in the United States than it was in the 1970s, making it the second leading cause of death for those between the ages of 10 and 24. Some statistics:

- In 2005, 5,686 people aged 10 to 24 were murdered in the United States — an average of 16 per day.
- Emergency rooms treated more than 720,000 violence-related injuries in people aged 10 to 24 in 2006.
- In a 2007 nationwide survey, 36 percent of high school students reported being in a physical fight during the preceding twelve months.
- In the 2007 survey, 18 percent of high school students reported they had taken a gun, knife, or club to school during the preceding thirty days.
- An estimated 30 percent of the nation's school kids between the sixth and tenth grades reported being involved in bullying.

Violence by the nation's youth has far-reaching social implications. It increases health care costs, decreases property values and productivity, and disrupts social services. The Children's Safety Network estimates the annual cost at more than $158 billion. The CDC's list of risk factors associated with youth violence reads like an indictment of the ills of society at large:

- prior history of being a victim of violent abuse
- drug, alcohol, or tobacco use
- friendships with delinquent peers
- poor family relations
- poor grades in school
- poverty in the community

After decades of rising youth violence, America faced a question in the 1980s that challenged its claims to being a country based on the ethics of natural law: Does such a society routinely kill its young? It took sixteen years to answer that fundamental question fully.

In 1989, citing "national standards of decency," the Supreme Court ended the practice of executing prisoners for murders committed at age sixteen. Oklahoma was the only state to execute such an offender while it was still legal.

In 1990, citing "contemporary standards of decency" the high court permitted states to execute inmates who committed their crimes at age seventeen. By 2005, citing the nation's same "contemporary standards of decency," the Supreme Court ruled that it was unconstitutional to execute murderers who killed at age seventeen. By that time, twenty-two such inmates had been executed in the twenty-five states that allowed the executions of seventeen-year-olds.

In 2001, Houston anti-death-penalty attorney Stanley Schneider pointed out to the *Houston Chronicle* that more than three hundred Texas laws called seventeen-year-olds minors. The laws forbade them to vote, join the army, drink legally, or consent to an abortion without parental permission.

"But a seventeen-year-old commits a crime, and they're thought to be mature enough to face the death penalty," Schneider said. "We all know seventeen-year-olds, many of them don't have the sense to come in out of the rain. We all know that seventeen-year-olds are mature one moment and act as children in the next. They don't understand the nature of their conduct. At what point does a child become an adult? Is it by virtue of their birthday?"

Harris County, of which Houston is the seat, lost the opportunity to execute more than two dozen juvenile killers whom it had sent to death row before the 2005 Supreme Court ruling outlawing the practice. But Texas's Family Code allows juveniles over the age of fifteen to be tried as adults, so Harris County has more than compensated for the Supreme Court ruling by trying and convicting half of the juvenile defendants in Texas as adults.

An October 2007 *Houston Chronicle* article reported that Harris County's disproportionate conviction rate of juveniles tried as adults occurred "despite youths here accounting for just 15 percent of all the juvenile crime in Texas, according to a review of state and local statistics."

During the past decade, Harris County has tried more juveniles as adults than Bexar, Dallas, Tarrant, and Travis counties combined, the newspaper reported. These counties contain Texas's other major cities: San Antonio, Dallas, Fort Worth, and Austin. The certification process involved in trying juveniles as adults has become so routine in Harris County that judges certify 90 percent of juveniles as adults in response to prosecutors' requests, according to the *Chronicle*. "Most juvenile offenders facing certification are poor, so their court-appointed attorneys, who struggle with heavy caseloads, may not have the time or resources to challenge prosecutors."

In 2002, the FBI reported, there were 16,200 murders in the United States. Juveniles were arrested in 1,360 of those cases, and 69 percent were charged with using a gun to kill their victims.

Sociologists offer a laundry list of reasons — critics call them "excuses" — to explain why some American children are so violent. But at least one factor — violence spewed from the entertainment industry through videos, music lyrics, computer games, movies, and the like — has produced a new breed of young criminals who have been weaned on a morality that gives fuel to the lawless ethic of "Mess with the best, die like the rest."

Criminal violence in children results from parental neglect and abuse, dysfunctional educational systems, morally bankrupt religious institutions, hopelessly corrupt political institutions, and unspeakably violent correctional institutions.

In April 1973, in an article in *Reader's Digest*, U.S. surgeon general Dr. Jesse Steinfeld estimated that 40 million children between the ages of two and eleven watched television an average of 3.5 hours per day and would see more than 100,000 incidences of violence and 13,400 simulated deaths before they reached the age of twelve.

A year after the Supreme Court outlawed executing inmates who committed murder at age seventeen, President George W. Bush signed into law the Adam Walsh Child Protection and Safety Act. Title I of the Walsh Act is called the Sex Offender Registration and Notification Act (SORNA). This section expanded the National Sex Offender Registry and established sentences of up to twenty years for sex offenders who don't comply with the law's registration requirements. It also requires that juveniles fourteen years of age or older convicted of sex crimes be treated in the same manner as adult sex offenders.

The states have until July 27, 2009, to implement the registration and notification standards set out under SORNA. Failure to comply will put a state at risk of losing 10 percent of federal Byrne Justice Assistance funds. While most states welcomed the 2006 enactment of SORNA, some now have questions about certain ramifications of the law, especially as they apply to juveniles. Prior to the Walsh Act, the only juveniles required to register as sex offenders were those who were prosecuted and convicted as adults.

Under SORNA, juveniles must register with local law enforcement either after conviction or upon release into the community. The public can then access significant personal information about them even though they are still minors.

Despite Texas's reputation for being tough on crime, it is one of an increasing number of states that have indicated they will ignore SORNA's mandate to register juvenile offenders. That decision comes from an unlikely coalition of law-and-order conservatives: victims' rights advocates, prosecutors, and "tough on crime" legislators. They believe that SORNA is too costly, unnecessarily strict, and can harm the victims it was designed to protect.

"We think our laws are strong enough," said

Senator Florence Shapiro, R-Plano, the legislature's leading proponent of sex offender registration, in a February 2008 *Houston Chronicle* article. And Bill Hawkins, chief of the juvenile division of the Harris County District Attorney's Office, agrees with her: "When the pendulum swings, it tends to swing hard. There are an awful lot of sexual assault cases, and then there are kids who engage in sex at an early age. The Adam Walsh Act wants to put them all together."

The U.S. Justice Department will eventually issue final guidelines that states must follow under the Walsh Act to remain eligible for federal funding. One of the Texas lawmakers who initially supported the act now opposes it because of its application to juvenile offenders and the cost of implementing it. Representative Jim McReynolds, D-Lufkin, told the *Chronicle* that it would cost local communities more to enact the SORNA requirements than they would receive in Byrne Justice Assistance funds.

"It's a financial loser . . . an unfunded mandate," McReynolds said.

While Texas has included juveniles in its sex offender registry for years, that inclusion was never automatic, because judges retained the discretion to decide who should be listed. The *Chronicle* reported that of the 47,000 sex offenders listed on the Department of Public Safety's Web site in 2007, only 275 are under the age of eighteen.

But the Walsh Act removes judicial discretion. It mandates that anyone fourteen years old or older, convicted of a sex offense, must register.

The *Chronicle* pointed out the potential harm the mandatory registration requirement poses. A fourteen-year-old boy convicted of having consensual sex with his twelve-year-old girlfriend would receive the same treatment as a "repeat adult predator who attacked a 3-year-old. Both would fall into the most severe category, Tier III, requiring them to register four times a year for at least 25 years and possibly for the rest of their lives."

"It's based on the offense of conviction and not on the risk level," said Allison Taylor, executive director of the Texas Council on Sex Offender Treatment.

Senator Shapiro and others stress that they are not soft on sex offenders, regardless of whether they fall into a low- or high-risk category. "I don't have any problem if they're adults," she said. "It's more difficult to change the behavior pattern of a thirty-five- or forty-year-old man."

The *Chronicle* cited studies that show that less than 10 percent of juveniles who commit sex offenses reoffend as adults. University of California law professor Franklin Zimring has also studied the issue. He found that, compared with juveniles who commit sex offenses, those who commit nonsexual offenses are twice as likely to become sex offenders as adults.

But not everyone wants to embrace a softer approach. Victims of sexual assaults by juveniles say the assaults are just as serious as adult assaults. And statistical data support the claim that juveniles have become more sexually active — and aggressive — over the last two decades.

So what's behind these statistics?

In 2001, the Rand Corporation conducted a study to determine the impact of sexually explicit music on the sexual behavior of teenagers between the ages of twelve and seventeen. The study involved 1,461 participants, most of whom had no prior sexual conduct. The results were startling. They revealed that 51 percent of the teens who said they listened to songs with explicit sexual lyrics — songs that portrayed men as studs and women as objects — were more likely to engage in sexual intercourse or other sexual activities within two years of listening to the lyrics, as opposed to 29 percent of those teens who did not listen to sexually explicit music.

The study's results appeared in *Pediatrics* in August 2006. Steven Martino, the lead author of the study, was quoted by Lindsey Tanner of the AP on August 6, 2006, as saying that exposure to sexually degrading music gave many teens a "specific message about sex" — boys learn to pursue girls relentlessly, and girls learn to view themselves as objects. "We think that really lowers kids' inhibitions and makes them less thoughtful" about sexual decisions, prompting many to engage in activity that they later regret, Martino said.

Natasha Ramsey, a seventeen-year-old New Jersey teen and an editor of SexEtc.org, a teen sexual health Web site produced at Rutgers University, told Tanner: "I won't really realize that the person is talking about having sex or raping a girl" in a song, but it "is being beaten into the teens' heads. We don't even realize how much. A lot of teens think that's the way they're supposed to be, they think that's the cool thing to do. Because it's so common, it's accepted. Teens will try to deny it, they'll say, 'No, it's not the music,' but it IS the music. That has one of the biggest impacts on our lives."

David Walsh, a psychologist who heads the National Institute on Media and the Family agreed, saying that without question music videos and other visual media directly influence human behavior. At the same time that hormones trigger sexual interest in a teenager, Walsh told Tanner, the brain's impulse-control center is undergoing "major construction." When sexually stimulating music mixes with the psychological and physical aspects of brain maturation and the developing sex drive, "it's not surprising that a kid with a heavier diet of [sexually explicit music] would be at greater risk for sexual behavior," Walsh said.

Martino said the Rand researchers tried to include the effect of parental permissiveness and other social factors on teens' sexual behavior but suggested that sexually explicit music had the greatest impact.

Leonard Pitts, a syndicated columnist for the *Miami Herald*, held the same opinion even before the Rand study appeared. On April 21, 2006, he wrote that violent sexual fantasies among teenagers have "seeped like sewage into our culture, showing up in that video game where you kill prostitutes and rob them, in that music video where a credit card is swiped through a woman's backside, in the defamation and death threats that greeted the young woman who accused Kobe Bryant of raping her."

In a 1994 case, the Georgia Supreme Court commented:

> In a recent study administered at 32 Georgia high schools, fully 46 percent of the freshman girls (generally aged 14 to 15) surveyed reported that they were sexually active. One in seven of the students polled said they had started having sex before age 13!
>
> The statistics make it clear that sexual behavior is becoming more common: one in ten seniors said they had sex before age 13, while one in six

freshmen said they had become sexually active before that age. A study of child welfare recipients indicated that 35 percent of the children in foster care, and 22 percent of those living at home, had had sexual intercourse before their thirteenth birthday. Another recent study shows that 20 percent of this country's young people who attend church had participated in some form of sexual experimentation by age 13. Even as early as 1982, in a survey of 160,000 teenagers regarding their feelings and experience with sexual matters, 31 percent of the 13 to 14 year olds surveyed reported that they had had sexual intercourse.

The Georgia court was not alone in 1994 in expressing concern about teenage sex. That year, the Louisiana Second Circuit Court of Appeals quoted Dr. Robert Coles, a psychiatrist at Harvard Medical School, about teenage sex: "What a child needs as much as food, clothing, and a good education, is a moral purpose. Children need something to live for, not to yield to gross materialism, aimless hedonism, and self-indulgence."

Clearly the young in America are becoming more sexually aggressive and therefore dangerous. In 2000, the Center for Sex Management in Silver Spring, Maryland, released a report entitled: *Adolescent Offenders: Myths/Facts about Juvenile Sex Offenders.* The study's findings show that the trend toward youthful sex crimes is increasing.

- One-fifth of all rapes and half of all child molestations in this country are committed by 13-to-17-year-olds.
- In 1995, approximately 18 adolescents per 100,000 were arrested for forcible rape.

- While these sex offenders are generally between 13 and 17 years of age, prepubescent youths also engaged in violent sexual behavior.
- Some 30–60 percent of juvenile sex offenders exhibit learning disabilities and academic dysfunction.
- Up to 80 percent have diagnosable psychiatric disorders.
- Many have problems with judgment and impulse control.
- One-fifth to one-half have a history of physical abuse, while 40–80 percent have a history of sexual abuse.

Another study in 2000, *Understanding Juvenile Sex Offenders: Research and Guidelines for Effective Management and Treatment*, conducted by the University of Virginia, supported the above study's results. Dr. J. A. Hunter opened the report with this observation:

> Juvenile perpetrated sexual aggression has been a problem of growing concern in American society over the past decade. Currently it is estimated that juveniles account for up to one-fifth of the rapes, and one-half of the cases of child molestation committed in the United States each year. The majority of cases of juvenile sexual aggression appear to involve adolescent male perpetrators; however, a number of clinical studies have pointed to the presence of females and prepubescent youths who have engaged in sexually abusive behaviors.

Dr. Hunter noted that the "developmental origin" of aggressive juvenile sexual behavior includes but is not limited to "maltreatment experiences, exposure to pornography, substance abuse, and exposure to aggressive role models."

The nation's criminal justice system must find a

swift, certain, and rational way to respond to these violent young offenders. Killing them is not an option. Trying them as adults, imposing harsh sentences, and placing them in state prisons ruled by gang violence, homosexual rape, and official corruption only reinforces the violent activity that sent them to prison in the first place.

Yet thirty-nine states have adopted policies of jailing the young in adult prisons with life sentences and no benefit of parole, according to a study by Northwestern University Law School's Children and Family Justice Center and the John Howard Association. These states — almost the entire Union — now incarcerate approximately 2,300 "kid lifers." Illinois enacted its kid-lifer law twenty years ago, but it has recently joined with California, Florida, Michigan, and Nebraska in trying to change it.

States should not be in the business of warehousing human beings for 40, 50, or even 60 years, long after brain maturation has probably ended their violent tendencies. To avoid the staggering costs of incarcerating youthful offenders for a half-century or more, the nation must rescue children victimized by domestic violence, sexual abuse, and drug abuse.

Juvenile predators mirror the soul of the society that produced them. They are born innocent. Society and circumstance transform them into predators. Public rants from law-and-order politicians and hate-filled demands for vengeance by crime victims' advocates are not the answer. They only fuel the cycle of violence.

As we have seen in recent years, America doesn't need more domestic wars. The war on terrorism, war on crime, war on juvenile crime, war on drugs, or even wars on poverty, teen pregnancy, truancy, domestic violence, and bullying cannot be won, and they promote slogans that produce no results. What we do need is to commit to responsible, honest action by our political, educational, and legal systems to produce a society whose young citizens respect law and order, due process, and equal protection of the law for all people.

The us-against-them mindset afflicting this nation — Democrats versus Republicans, liberals versus conservatives, Christians versus Muslims, color versus color — intractably produces mistrust, hatred, and violence. It creates a society as fraught with tension, paranoia, and corruption as the keeper-versus-kept society inside our prisons.

No nation that abandons its young can expect to live without fearing them. Look again at the statement that Sean Derrick O'Brien made as a thirty-year-old man, the year before his execution for raping and murdering two young girls when he was eighteen years old: "I wonder how many children could be saved or kept living, who would otherwise die, with the monies states use to kill men and women on death row. . . . We bear the responsibility of showing our children how to be human, and if we can't our world will continue to suffer for it. Life is a miracle and therefore precious. Each time one is taken before its time, the world loses something special."

We do bear the responsibility of showing our children how to be human. So far, we have failed.

14

The Saga of Louisiana's First Post-*Furman* Execution

"A nigger mess."

That's what some cops in the Houston Police Department in the 1960s called black-on-black murder. The blatant bigotry of that era is apparent today in national death penalty statistics. For thirty-two years, in the post-*Furman* era from 1977 through November 30, 2008, the number of blacks put to death for murdering blacks lagged far behind those executed for killing whites. The death penalty is reserved usually for cases involving socially established white people.

Of the 1,135 offenders put to death in the United States during that period, 79 percent were executed for killing whites, 14 percent for killing blacks, and 5 percent for killing Hispanics — all while justice wore her blindfold.

A 1991 *New York Times* article, "White Dies for Killing Black, for First Time in Decades," reported that of the nearly 15,000 executions carried out in this nation's history, only 31 white people had been executed for killing a black person or people.

Since that *Times* article, another 14 white offenders were put to death for killing a black victim and 229 black offenders were put to death for killing white victims while another 119 black offenders were put to death for killing black victims.

So what set of facts and circumstances earn the death penalty for a black killer with a black victim?

Robert Wayne Williams, a black man, was among the 14 percent put to death for killing another black person. He was not only a black man put to death for killing a black victim, he was the first man executed in Louisiana since 1961, putting an end to the *Furman* moratorium in that state. Of all the articles I wrote during my nine years on the *Angolite*'s staff while I did time at Angola, the one about Williams in 1983, entitled "The Execution," was the toughest.

I interviewed Williams several weeks before his death. He didn't say much, and when he spoke it was in a barely audible voice. He talked about the death penalty in general terms and referred me to his mother and his minister for "on the record" comments. After interviewing his mother, Rosella Williams, who was very gracious, I had to suppress certain facts.

The *Angolite* article focused on Williams's trial and execution, both a travesty of justice. But there was an additional aspect to the Williams case that was not presented in my article: the political corruption that fueled both the need and the speed of his execution. Rosella Williams and Williams's minister, Reverend J. D. Brown, both alluded to it when I interviewed them for the prison newsmagazine. However, I was a prisoner, and while the *Angolite* was uncensored for the most part, the dark hand of Louisiana politics remained off limits for an inmate writer. Today, as a free man, I can finally write about the ugly political conspiracy and the legal travesty that I saw so clearly in the 1980s from behind Angola's bars.

The power brokers of Baton Rouge and their friendly historians will say no connection links the staggering political events of 1983 and the Robert Wayne Williams execution. But Williams was clearly a scapegoat for a politician desperately trying save his career in the midst of an ugly scandal.

Williams's crime horrified Baton Rouge. He and his accomplice, Ralph Holmes, robbed an A&P grocery store in a popular shopping mall crowded with affluent customers on the night of January 5, 1979. The two men walked into the store wearing ski masks, and Williams came armed with a sawed-off shotgun. A sixty-seven-year-old security guard named Willie Kelly was bagging groceries when the robbers approached. Holmes tried to take Kelly's holstered gun, and the old man's hand moved toward the weapon.

"Don't try it!" Williams yelled as he pulled the trigger, striking Kelly in the face at point-blank range with a shotgun blast.

Kelly flew backward, dead before his body hit the floor. Williams and Holmes proceeded with the robbery. Some of the money they grabbed from the cashier fell to the floor. As Williams laid the shotgun down to pick up the money, the weapon discharged, striking several customers in the legs and feet. Amid the screams of terror and pain, Holmes pistol-whipped one of the customers before he and Williams fled into the night.

Then Assistant District Attorney John Sinquefield arrived at the supermarket shortly after the robbery to assist the police in their investigation. Wounded and terrified witnesses needed treatment, calming, and questioning. Nothing could be done for Kelly, whose faceless body lay on the floor in a cooling pool of blood.

Sinquefield studied the repulsive scene. There were no leads or any real evidence to indicate who had committed the crime.

Several weeks of investigation left the police even more frustrated, and it appeared the crime would go unsolved. Then they received a telephone call from an informant who named Williams and Holmes.

Shortly after his arrest, Williams gave the police a videotaped confession. Sinquefield watched the interrogation through a two-way mirror, listening to Williams confess. On April 10, 1979, three months after the robbery and murder, Williams went on trial before an all-white jury in Baton Rouge. Sinquefield asked for the death penalty.

Sinquefield told the jury that the Kelly murder had been carried out in cold blood. Williams, he said, planned the robbery, borrowed the shotgun, leveled it at Kelly, and deliberately blew the security guard's face off. The prosecutor stressed that Williams told Holmes to "get all the money," whereupon Holmes forced another clerk to open a cash register to get more money. Later that same night, the two robbers participated in a poker game in New Orleans during which Williams joked about killing the guard.

Williams's court-appointed attorneys argued that the shotgun was defective, saying it accidentally discharged and that their client didn't intend to kill Kelly. A weapons expert testified that the gun could have accidentally discharged. Williams didn't take the witness stand to tell the jury his intent.

The jury found Williams guilty and recommended the death penalty. His case moved up and down the state and federal judicial appeals ladder three times, appearing in twelve courts before the Supreme Court rejected his final application for a writ of certiorari on September 8, 1983. It took slightly more than four years to complete that judicial odyssey — a remarkably short period of time compared to other capital cases in Louisiana going through the same appeal process.

Sadness pervaded death row at the Louisiana State Penitentiary following the rejection of Williams's appeal in September 1983. Just six days earlier, Mississippi had executed Jimmy Lee Gray, the first man to walk into that state's death chamber in nineteen years. Death row inmates across the country had anticipated a swift resurgence in executions after the Supreme Court handed down a decision in the Texas death penalty case of Thomas Andy Barefoot, which cleared the way for the lower federal courts to accelerate the death penalty appeal process.

Like so many of his fellow condemned inmates, Williams was poor and lacked legal counsel after the Supreme Court rejected his final appeal. His former attorney, Richard Shapiro, an anti–death penalty attorney in New Orleans, had moved to New Jersey during the appeal process. Williams's only hope for a lawyer lay with Louisiana's anti–death penalty groups. His family had no money to hire an attorney to handle the expensive litigation involved in a last-ditch effort to save his life.

Like sharks circling for the kill, the Baton Rouge justice system moved swiftly at the smell of blood. State district court judge Frank Foil issued a new death warrant less than two weeks after the final Supreme Court rejection. It marked the fourth time Williams had been given a death date. This time the execution was set for October 25, 1983.

The NAACP Legal Defense Fund implored Sam Dalton, an experienced death penalty attorney, to go to Williams's aid until it could locate another attorney to represent him. Williams had never met Dalton.

"Because Shapiro had moved out of state," Dalton said, "I was simply asked to sign some pleadings as a convenience and courtesy to the NAACP Defense Fund. That was like putting my toe in quicksand. Suddenly I was up to my neck, facing an October twenty-fifth death date — and as things grew more desperate, I was drawn more into the case, from signing pleadings as a matter of courtesy to carrying the whole load."

Dalton filed a standardized habeas corpus petition and an application for a stay of execution in the state district court on October 4. Judge Foil denied the applications that same day. On October 13, the Louisiana Supreme Court also rejected Williams's bid for a stay. He had just seven days until his scheduled execution.

A quiet and intelligent man, Williams played chess and read to keep his mind off his impending death. He also spent many hours on bended knees in silent prayer. Death row had given him ample time to evaluate his life.

During those frantic deathwatch days, when the fear of dying paralyzed his thoughts, Williams reached out to the troubled young people attending his mother's church. He wrote letters to them about how futile a life of crime is and how drugs inevitably lead to violence and ruin.

Alone on a steel bunk, Williams examined his own life. It wasn't pretty. He had left Sunday school at age thirteen to join the criminal world of hard drugs, fast women, and proverbial easy living. He became part of the lowest ranks of the Baton Rouge social order, a by-product of the city's flourishing cocaine industry. The drug saturated the state capital, destroying lives. Infamous DEA informant Barry Seal smuggled it into the city, and some of the city's most prominent residents were users.

On October 20, 1983, Dalton filed a habeas corpus and stay application in federal court before U.S. District Court judge Frank Polozola. Like his predecessor and proponent of the death penalty, Judge E. Gordon West, Polozola wasn't about to block the execution. He staunchly advocated the death penalty.

"This court does not believe [it] is required to stay all proceedings herein pending a decision by the U.S. Supreme Court in [another] case," Polozola said.

"I think that is what they were doing," Rosella Williams said. "I can't understand why they pushed his case so fast above other cases that had been there longer."

Those cases came from different parts of the state. Politics weren't involved there, but District Attorney Ossie Brown needed a law-and-order win to deflect attention from his impending federal indictment on corruption charges. He needed to restore the normal order

of southern crime to restore his reputation. Robert
Wayne Williams was political serendipity.

The case also involved substantial constitutional issues. Williams never received an evidentiary hearing on
any of those issues, even though dissenting judges at both
the state and federal levels voted in favor of holding hear-
ings to consider the issues — a clear indication that his
case was raising serious legal questions.

The decisions by the courts not to hear these issues
and the extraordinary judicial speed with which they
were reviewed raises suspicion. Judge Foil, the Louisiana
Supreme Court, and Judge Polozola denied Williams's
first round of postconviction appeals in three days. No
capital case in Louisiana's entire history had ever trav-
eled so swiftly through the first round of the postconviction process. Yet in 1983 Judge Polozola said that
Williams had received an "exhaustive review" of his constitutional claims.

Williams's spiritual advisor, Reverend J. D. Brown,
pastor of the Faith Chapel Church of God, also believed
that the case had been deliberately and ruthlessly rushed
through the appeals process. "Now, why Mr. [Ossie]
Brown wanted to execute Robert Wayne Williams remains a question in my mind," he said. "Why did he pick
that particular case out? I don't know — but I do know I
was told that Robert was going to die in 1983. A rep-
utable person in politics told me that he was going to die,
that there would be an execution before 1983 was out
and Robert would be the one executed."

The day after Judge Polozola denied Williams's
stay request, Dalton filed a motion for a stay with the
Fifth Circuit Court of Appeals. The appeals court stayed

the execution on October 23 but deviated from its normal procedure by simultaneously upholding Polozola's ruling.

Death row inmates oscillate between the joy of a stay and the bitter disappointment of a denial. News of the Fifth Circuit stay brought relief to Williams's dark world. He felt drained and depleted. The deathwatch was over — if only for the moment.

Ossie Brown, however, wasn't about to accept the Fifth Circuit's ruling. He knew that Chief Justice Warren Burger was trying to make it clear to lower courts that the death penalty was an acceptable reality in America, so Brown filed a request with the Supreme Court to lift the Fifth Circuit stay. On November 7, the high court complied.

The Supreme Court sealed Williams's fate. There was no way for him to avoid execution now. Paralyzed with fear, he sat alone in his death cell trying to digest the news. He clung desperately to the hope that another judge in another court would save him.

His attorney, Sam Dalton, could have walked away from the case at that point. The Supreme Court had spoken the final word. But Dalton had committed himself to one of the most courageous battles a man can wage: a fight to stop the state from ending a life. Judge Foil, determined to see that power exercised, set Williams's new death date for December 14. Williams wouldn't see another Christmas.

Dalton, it must be stated, didn't feel that Williams should escape punishment. He believed only that it was fundamentally unfair to execute Williams when murderers who had committed more heinous crimes received life sentences. That paradox impelled Dalton to make an extraordinary request for clemency to the governor of Louisiana. Nine state and federal judges had consistently dissented in the case. All held the opinion that Williams's death sentence was inappropriate. In an unusual move, Governor David Treen's pardon board granted Williams a hearing.

Dalton had never read Williams's trial transcript, but he did so in preparation for the clemency hearing. That Williams hadn't testified at his own trial; that his lawyers didn't let him tell the jury his intent; that he had no opportunity to say that the shotgun had accidentally discharged—all struck Dalton as a miscarriage of justice.

"When I went to death row to talk with Robert Wayne," Dalton said, "I asked him why he hadn't taken the stand and talked to the jury. He told me his lawyer told him they were not going to use him and for him to keep quiet."

Dalton was outraged. Had Williams testified in his own defense, Dalton believed, as he stated in his *Angolite* interview, he wouldn't have received the death penalty.

> You have to understand what the defense attorneys were doing. Their defense was a lack of specific intent to kill. That's called, of course, a state-of-mind defense. Now, there are two kinds of state-of-mind defenses. First, there is the kind where you plead insanity, but the attorneys did not plead insanity. So when you don't plead insanity, you can't sell your intent by the use of psychiatrists and doctors; you can't even use those experts unless you're talking about a plea of insanity.
>
> So, when you are using the kind of state-of-mind defense used by Williams's attorneys, guess

who your best witness is. That's right — the defendant. The jury needs that evidence; it needs to hear that best evidence. They needed to hear this man get up on that witness stand and say, "Look, I didn't intend to do this — I robbed, I kicked somebody's shins, I ran off with the money, but I didn't intend to kill." All you need is for one juror to identify with that.

The state trial court had appointed two attorneys to represent Williams. One was blind, and the other had less than five years' experience. (An attorney in Louisiana must have at least five years of experience before he can defend a capital case alone.) They didn't stand a chance against Sinquefield.

Dalton held that

Those attorneys didn't do a good job. They concentrated on trying to establish their defense that the gun accidentally discharged through a very weak expert. They should have done a much better job on that. If they were going to choose that defense, they should have demonstrated it with Williams's testimony, but they chose to concentrate solely on the condition of the shotgun. That was a very, very weak way of proving lack of intent, especially when your best evidence is sitting right there next to you. There was no reason not to use him. Even assuming that there was some reason to keep him off the stand during the guilt or innocence phase of the trial, there was absolutely no reason known to man to keep him off the stand during the penalty phase. Simply putting a man on the stand and letting him plead for his life sometimes is enough for a juror to vote life instead of death. None of this was done.

And Reverend Brown agreed with Dalton. "I talked to the attorney that represented Robert," the pastor said. "I told that attorney the one thing he should do was put Robert on the stand and let him talk about that he did not intend to do it. I consulted with the attorney for a long time about the case, and I was there at the trial. I just didn't feel like the attorney was competent enough to represent him, the blind one. I don't know — it was just lacking somewhere."

Neither Judge Foil nor Judge Polozola had the constitutional issue of ineffective assistance of counsel presented to him.

On December 5, 1983, the Louisiana Board of Pardons heard Williams's plea for clemency. Dalton couldn't argue that Williams's lawyers were ineffective because the courts had never entertained the issue. Dalton had only one issue he could present: mitigation. He could argue only that Williams hadn't intended to kill Willie Kelly.

Reverend Brown attended the hearing and pled another issue: forgiveness.

Robert was a Sunday school scholar of the Faith Chapel Church of God, but he drifted out of Sunday school and picked up with the wrong crowd. He stopped coming to church. He would only come to visit now and then. My real contact with Robert came after he committed this crime. A group of people came to see me and said Robert was in trouble. I went to see him in the jailhouse, and I've followed him since. He admitted to me that he committed the crime, and he said he was sorry for it. He told me it was an accident and that he was very, very sorry. He was in misery for six weeks while I was visiting him at the parish prison. It was there that he accepted the Lord Jesus Christ as his personal savior and I baptized him. He cried and cried and said that if he could undo anything, he would undo his crime. He was sincere and sorry for what he done.

His mother made an emotional plea for her son's life. Tragedy hung heavy in the air as she spoke. His sister and son became too emotional to finish their pleas for mercy. The victim's family sat in one section of the room in soft blue chairs. The Williams family sat in hard red chairs. The contrast was sharp and obvious.

Then Williams addressed the board:

This is the worst tragedy of my life. It's caused a lot of pain and suffering to the victim's family, to my family, and to me. When I was raised, I never wanted anyone's life to be taken by my hands. I had no intention of killing anyone that night. The gun had shells in it, but the guys who gave it to me said it wasn't in working order — that it wouldn't fire. But the gun discharged — it fired so fast. I live it every day. I wake up and pray for my family. I pray for the victim's family and hope that we can both come together. I wish that this had never happened — if there's anyone in this world who wishes he could turn this thing around, it's me. God only knows what the future holds — I just want the Kelly family to know that from my heart I am very sorry.

The Kelly family showed no hatred of Williams. Charles Kelly, a career officer with the Louisiana Department of Corrections and Willie Kelly's son, addressed the board on behalf of the family:

> I think there was a clear intent to kill my father. He was a very small man, about five-foot-four and weighed about 135 pounds. They could have easily manhandled him. Even if our father had tried to grab him [Williams], I think Mr. Holmes could have grabbed him. Like I said, he was small — he didn't have to shoot him, and if he had to shoot him, he didn't have to shoot him in the face. . . . I respect the courts and all their proceedings. I think they were conducted fairly and impartially up to this point. As a law-abiding, tax-paying citizen, it seems only fair to me that the judgment be carried out. I just want to say to the Williams family and to Robert that I mean no ill will. My daddy is gone and I have a little son who will never see his grandfather.

Kelly's words trailed off as he got up and walked away from the board. It was a dramatic, powerful moment. He was drowning in grief.

Then Ossie Brown addressed the board. "The American public distrusts the justice system because we're not carrying out the intent of the law," Brown told the pardon board. "My office did not single out Robert Wayne Williams and put a crime on him that he did not intend to commit. He killed a good, law-abiding citizen. It was a heinous, vicious crime, and we cannot excuse it."

Brown was not pitching his words to the pardon

board alone. He was facing a federal criminal indictment on the charge that he had taken a bribe from a prominent Baton Rouge businessman, James D'Spain, to influence another case. The media, Brown knew, were watching him intently. And so was much of Louisiana.

That other case, the Glen D'Spain and Dr. Kraemer Diel case, began on August 19, 1982, when Baton Rouge detective Robert Howle and city police officer Bill Brogan approached a $40,000 Mercedes-Benz parked in an alley behind Murphy's Lounge in the LSU Shopping Center. The car was parked in an unusual manner with its brake lights on. As the detective approached the driver's side of the vehicle, he saw a man later identified as Dr. Kraemer Diel, a dentist with the LSU Athletic Department, holding a piece of paper with a white substance on it. The detective drew his gun and ordered Diel out of the vehicle.

Brogan had approached the other side of the vehicle and ordered the second man out of the car. That second man was Glen D'Spain, son of businessman James D'Spain. Near him, Brogan saw a baggie containing white powder lying on the floor of the car.

The officers arrested and booked the two men with possession for intent to distribute ten grams of cocaine. The two men quickly posted bond and left jail. At first, it looked like a run-of-the-mill case: two socially prominent men caught doing cocaine. But it quickly morphed into one of the biggest stories in Baton Rouge in 1983, exposing serious narcotics trafficking and political corruption in Louisiana's capital.

In June of that year, a grand jury refused to indict young D'Spain on cocaine charges. The next day, James D'Spain loaned $134,000 to an ice cream company

owned by Ossie Brown, Baton Rouge mayoral aide David
Bourland, and city civil director Larry Gibbens.

Presumably acting upon information supplied to
him by state law enforcement officials, Assistant U.S. Attorney Stanford Bardwell promptly announced that a
federal grand jury was investigating the circumstances
surrounding the D'Spain loan. Brown and Bourland
quickly denied any wrongdoing, saying they were first
approached by James D'Spain in May 1982 about the
loan. When the younger D'Spain and Diel were arrested,
Brown said, he immediately called Bourland and told
him not to go through with the loan. The story went that
Bourland didn't follow Brown's suggestion.

The ice cream company, Beverly Hills Confections,
formed in 1980, had opened for business in the spring of
1981 and folded that same year. The $134,000 D'Spain
loan covered some of the $200,000 that Brown, Bour-
land, and Gibbens had invested in the financial mis-
adventure.

After the charge against young D'Spain was dismissed, Bourland said, he felt free to follow through with
the loan and he signed Brown's name to the document.

Shortly after the news about Bardwell's investigation broke, WBRZ-TV revealed that the Mercedes-Benz
belonged to a company owned by local millionaire
Claude Pennington III. State law allowed for vehicles involved in the transportation of drugs to be seized, but in
a departure from normal procedures, the Mercedes was
released the day after the D'Spain–Diel arrest to Jerry
Kennison, a former Baton Rouge deputy sheriff and former state police detective then employed by Pennington's company. City police chief Pat Bonnano, who had
been in Florida when the D'Spain–Diel arrest occurred,

justified the release of the car by saying that Howle and Brogan were not narcotics officers and didn't know that a hold could have been placed on the vehicle.

As the news cycle took up the Pennington connection to the Mercedes, Brown filed a motion in state court saying that he was stepping out of the prosecution of D'Spain and Diel to "avoid even the appearance of impropriety." Brown also held a meeting with his staff to announce he was changing the locks on the doors to his office, saying that it was necessary because records checked out to him had turned up in the offices of other assistants. Changing the locks, he said, ensured that nothing could be removed from his office without his or his secretary's knowledge.

Then Brown took an abrupt leave of absence. Bourland followed the district attorney's surprising decision with the public revelation that Claude Pennington III owned 25 percent of Beverly Hills Confections, contradicting previous statements to the media. Bourland said he had not mentioned Pennington's involvement because "I didn't see any reason to involve an innocent person."

So why did Brown and Bourland need to borrow money from James D'Spain when they already had a wealthy partner like Claude Pennington? Bourland responded that Pennington had bought a 25 percent interest in the company for $25,000 so he would be eligible for a portion of the tax credits from the original $200,000 that Brown, Bourland, and Gibbens had invested.

A little more than a week after Bardwell announced the federal probe of the D'Spain–Diel case, Bourland resigned from his position in Mayor Pat Screen's office, where he had been making more money than the mayor himself and where, after Mayor Screen had been hospitalized in 1981 for substance abuse, Bourland took over daily operations.

The same day that Bourland tendered his resignation, Louisiana attorney general William Guste announced that his office would turn over prosecution of the D'Spain–Diel case to federal authorities. "We both believe that the best interests of law enforcement would be served by taking this action," Guste said. "This case and our decision as to its treatment is a good illustration of the continuing cooperation that we believe is important to good law enforcement."

Less than two weeks after Bardwell's probe began, a federal grand jury indicted Glen D'Spain and Kraemer Diel for possession with intent to distribute cocaine.

Bardwell said the federal indictment was based on the information from Ossie Brown's office. "We presented evidence that came from the arresting officers. I don't know what they [Brown's office] presented to their grand jury."

Bardwell also said that his office was amenable to a plea bargain "under the right circumstances if we are provided something in exchange."

Several days after the announcement of the latest indictments, Brown returned from his "vacation" and met with reporters.

"I have served the people of this parish for the past eleven years to the very best of my ability," he said. "Never before, in my private practice or as district attorney of this parish for these many years, has my honesty or integrity ever been questioned. . . . I would never do anything to discredit this office, myself, my family, or the people of this parish."

In September 1983, federal authorities also indicted

Claude Pennington III on a charge of possession of cocaine, to which he entered a guilty plea. The indictment and plea agreement identified him as the supplier of the cocaine in the Glen D'Spain and Kraemer Diel case.

Pennington retained prominent criminal defense attorney Bryan Bush to represent him in the federal criminal proceedings. Bush informed the media that he had been negotiating the plea agreement with federal authorities for several months. He said his client had been cooperating with the federal grand jury probe of the $134,000 loan from James D'Spain to Brown and Bourland.

With Pennington's cooperation, the FBI began checking state court records of several cases handled by Brown's office, primarily drug cases that had not been prosecuted.

"Any agent is free to look at any records of this office for the past eleven years," Ossie Brown said. "The cases in this office have been handled proper and according to law and are public and available to anyone. For eleven years this office has been conducted in the interest of the public, and all actions taken have been done in what the assistant district attorneys and I feel are in the best interest and fair determination of all the people of this parish."

The local court clerk said that the record search was not random. FBI agents came with specific names and cases. They also spoke to several judges in connection with their probe.

"I have no idea what cases they are looking at," Brown informed the media. "We will be happy to help them with any cases they are looking at. This office operates with an open door policy."

A week later, five members of Brown's office, including his personal secretary, were subpoenaed before the federal grand jury. Brown couldn't explain the subpoenas.

"We are cooperating," he said. "Anything they want to know about, we are helping. There has been no wrongdoing in this office. Everything is above board. Our people are willing to cooperate in any investigation."

An FBI agent and a state police detective, who were part of a special task force under the federally funded Organized Crime Drug Enforcement Task Force, served those subpoenas. That task force had been assigned to investigate not only the Glen D'Spain and Kraemer Diel case but other drug cases handled by Brown's office. Local law enforcement believed that organized crime elements were influencing Brown's office.

Ossie Brown realized that matters were spiraling out of control. In mid-October 1983, he appeared before the federal grand jury. His testimony lasted four hours. He emerged from the session arrogant and confident as always, telling reporters that he had answered every question put to him. But Brown's cocky attitude disappeared several weeks later when his personal secretary, Marian Whitaker, was indicted on two counts of lying to the federal grand jury.

"I adhere to the philosophy that a person is innocent until proven guilty," Brown said in a prepared statement, "and I see no reason why I should veer from that in this case. I am confident that she will be exonerated in this matter. Marian and her family have my best wishes and prayers."

Then one of Brown's key assistants, Richard Johnson, suddenly resigned. He joined others who had also resigned. One of them, Premilla Chumley, had joined Bardwell's staff.

It was in the midst of these stunning political developments that Ossie Brown seized on the Williams case and ruthlessly used it to shore up his law-and-order image.

And it was in this highly charged political atmosphere that Brown told the pardon board, "The American public distrusts the justice system because we're not carrying out the intent of the law. My office did not single out Robert Wayne Williams and put a crime on him that he did not intend to commit."

The next day, the pardon board voted 3 to 2 to deny clemency for Williams. Two days later, bolstered by the votes of two pardon board members to grant Williams clemency, a Baton Rouge and New Orleans coalition called the Religious Leaders Against the Death Penalty urged Governor David Treen to grant mercy in Williams case.

"Redemption is what we are asking of Governor Treen," said Tim Lawson, a Methodist minister from Istrouma. "Rehabilitation, renewal of the life of Robert Wayne Williams."

But Governor Treen refused to meet with these diverse religious groups.

"In this holiday season of grace," Reverend Steve Crump told the media, "we will opt for the religion of decency, or we will opt for the religion of vengeance, the religion of King Herod."

Herod's religion prevailed. Governor Treen didn't grant the plea for clemency.

Williams had a final telephone conversation with

Dalton. "I want to thank you and all the people who worked with you for everything you did," the inmate said. "I really appreciate it — and I'm not going to let y'all down. I'm going to handle this thing with a lot of dignity — and I want you to know I am going to die with the truth in my heart, the truth that I didn't intend to kill anyone."

On December 13, the last full day of Robert Williams's life, he sat in Camp F, one of the remote satellite units spread across Angola's 18,000 acres and the site of the prison's death chamber. A blanket covered the window. What began as a fair day turned ugly as the other inmates marched to the dining hall for their noon meal. The sky suddenly grew so dark that the prison had to turn on the nighttime security lights. Lightning bolts cracked the black sky, and thunder boomed above. It made everyone nervous. Rain began but then stopped. The sky lightened, and the security lights were turned off.

Sam Dalton moved from one court to another, from one judge to another. He knew the system was going to kill his client, but that didn't stop his efforts. "That last issue was a good issue," Dalton said, referring to the intent issue. "But the courts said it came too late. Now, that goes against the grain of the writ of habeas corpus. I don't care if you file a hundred habeas corpus petitions and ninety-nine of them are bad, when you file a good one, it should be honored. It shouldn't make any difference when it's filed."

Then Dalton put it this way:

Since the state and federal constitutions prohibit the suspension of the writ of habeas corpus, the courts have found a trick, a piece of terminology, to get around that constitutional safeguard. It's called "abuse of the writ." They say, "Well, we can't talk in terms of suspension, so we'll talk in terms of abuse" which, in effect, is a suspension of the writ. That's what the Fifth Circuit did on the last issue in Williams's case. They said it should have been brought up earlier and by bringing it up at that late hour, it was an abuse of the writ.

A week earlier in another Louisiana death penalty case, in which a white inmate had brutally murdered an elderly woman in New Orleans, the Fifth Circuit stayed his scheduled execution and ordered a hearing on an abuse-of-the-writ issue he presented to the court. But the Fifth Circuit deviated from its own case law by summarily denying Williams's same claim.

As Dalton saw it,

They should have ordered a hearing in Williams's case. There was absolutely no reason for them not to order such a hearing. We had presented a good solid issue. Their decision hurt — it hurt the legal system, the judicial process, because they ignored the strength of the Great Writ. Despite the constitutional prohibition that they shouldn't, they used a trick of terminology to suspend the writ of habeas corpus by calling it an abuse instead of a suspension. The fact is that they suspended it.

That Tuesday afternoon, Governor Treen issued a statement rejecting the plea for mercy made by the state's religious leaders: "I have reviewed and given careful and prayerful consideration to the many arguments that have been advanced by those who seek clemency for Robert

Wayne Williams. I do not find that the judicial system has failed or that there is any other justification for the extraordinary clemency power given the governor. It is my decision not to grant a reprieve or commutation of sentence."

That night, as the waiting reporters and witnesses prepared for the death ritual, the sky suddenly grew dark again. Heavy rain fell, whipped about in a crisscross frenzy by unusually high winds. Lightning flashed across the sky, filling the black night with veins of intense light. For half an hour, the turbulent storm unleashed its raging fury over the prison. Then, just as suddenly as it had hit the prison, the storm stopped. An ominous silence ensued.

"These white folks are crazy," a tense black correctional officer said. "They don't understand this weather. They think it's a storm. But that's the Lord letting them know He doesn't like what they're about to do here. It's evil—and you can feel it, the air is full of it. And it ain't got nothin' to do with the death penalty. This is about that dude over there and the people who want to kill him. There's something that ain't right about this thing. They can call it a storm if they want, but it ain't natural."

Some thirty demonstrators braved the weather to protest Williams's execution, singing and praying for the soul of the condemned man.

"I guess we are praying for a miracle," said Tom Dyhdahl, a spokesman for Louisiana Citizens Against the Death Penalty. Nick Trenticosta, a spokesman for the Louisiana Coalition on Jails and Prisons, added, "We're also praying that everybody else on death row there and elsewhere in this country will not face the same fate as Robert Wayne Williams."

The Williams family joined the protestors.

Reverend Joe Ingles, standing with them, also took note of the weather, saying, "The total darkness speaks well of the shame we're witnessing here tonight."

While the protestors sang hymns, Sam Dalton searched frantically for a proverbial needle in the judicial haystack. Everywhere he turned, doors slammed shut in his face.

At 10:30 P.M. the lights in the prison went out, signaling an end to the day. Reverend Brown was sitting in front of Williams's death cell. He had been talking to the troubled inmate about many matters from his childhood to adulthood.

> He had a problem understanding how inadequate, how unfair the justice system is. He didn't understand why Mr. Treen, who is a Christian, didn't step in and stop the execution. I had to show Robert that Mr. Treen had his own convictions, that he was following the law, that he had sent his pardon board to the prison to hear his case, and that two of those board members voted for clemency.
>
> The next thing that bothered Robert was the fact that there had always been judges, even the two pardon board members, who had voted for him, that it had never been a unanimous vote to see him executed. "Why don't they stop this thing," he said. "Why me? Why doesn't someone stop this and see I didn't intend to kill Mr. Kelly?" But I was able to calm him down — and we went over the Psalms again.

At approximately 11:30, as they were talking, Williams suddenly told Reverend Brown, "Stop! I want you to cease saying anything else. Get me ready to die. I want you to really prepare me to walk into Heaven. I want you to tell me what it's really like — tell me what I can expect when I get there."

Reverend Brown began to prepare Williams for death by taking him through the Psalms again. As he recounted it: "We began to repeat the Lord's Prayer — and when we got to 'forgive me my trespasses, as I forgive those who trespass against me,' we paused and he repeated it over and over again. He said that 'in order for God to forgive me, I've got to get everything clear in my mind.' Then he said, 'Thank you for letting me get that clear,' and at that point he said, 'I don't hold nothing against Mr. Treen or anybody else.'"

At 12:45 A.M. guards entered Williams's cell and placed shackles around his ankles and handcuffs on his wrists.

Then, Reverend Brown said,

Robert began repeating the Lord's Prayer again, and then he stopped repeating it and followed me in repeating the Twenty-third Psalm. A halo came over him, and he was not himself. He said these words to me: "You've talked to me about Jesus bearing my burdens, that Jesus is going to sit in that chair instead of me." He paused and said, "I definitely believe and feel that it won't be me going to the chair — I believe that Jesus is going for me." When I saw that halo, I knew he had become embodied in Christ.

At 1:00 A.M. Warden Ross Maggio walked into Williams's cell. "Robert, it's time for us to go," he said.

The warden led the procession down the tier, down the hallway, through a lobby, and into another hallway that led to the death chamber. Reverend Brown accompanied the procession until it reached the witness room, at which point he had to leave Williams and join the other witnesses.

Williams and his guards took several more steps down the narrow hallway before turning right into the death chamber. The huge, crudely built electric chair sat waiting in the middle of the room. High above the chair, on the wall behind it, the hands of a large clock registered the time. Next to it, an exhaust fan waited to suck the stench of death from the room. A rectangular window gave witnesses a view of the proceedings.

Two prison guards and the warden escorted Williams to a podium inside the death chamber to make his final statement. Two other guards remained outside the closed chamber door. Williams looked directly at the witnesses, while Warden Maggio held the microphone as Williams spoke. In a firm, strong voice he said:

> I believe and feel deeply in my heart that God has come into my life and saved me. I told the truth about what happened. If my death do happen, I would like it to be a remembrance for Louisiana and the whole country that it would be a deterrence against capital punishment and show that capital punishment is no good and never has been good. I would like all the people who fought against capital punishment to keep on fighting not just on my behalf but on behalf of everyone else.

Behind Williams, in a small concrete enclosure that shielded him from view, the executioner waited. No one could see the man who was paid $400 to pull the switch.

A small opening in the wall allowed him to see the warden's signal to start the execution.

After Williams finished his statement, he turned, walked to the electric chair, and sat down. Two guards tightened the straps around him — one around his chest and the other for his left leg where an electrode was attached. They secured his right leg, then one arm after the other. Williams watched the two guards quizzically as they readied him for death.

The guards placed the cranial electrode on the top of Williams's head. Then, as a leather hood was being lowered over his face, Williams asked the warden if it was necessary.

"Yes, Robert, we have to use it," the warden replied.

The room fell deathly quiet. It had taken four minutes and twenty seconds to walk from the holding cell to reach that point in the death chamber. Maggio nodded to the executioner, who pulled the switch, sending 2,000 volts of electricity surging through Williams's body. The executioner lowered the surge to 500 volts for ten seconds, then increased it again to 2,000 volts before lowering it once more to 500 volts.

Killing Robert Williams took exactly one minute and ten seconds.

Reverend Brown later said:

> As I looked at that execution, there was a strong anger coming deep from within. As I watched Robert being executed, I realized that we, all of us here in America, are guilty of his death. We legalize alcohol and let our big politicians, our millionaires, control the drug traffic in this country, and it's them, if anyone, who should be electrocuted —

not the person who is down at the bottom. We only execute the ones down at the bottom, the ones who can't afford a lawyer, the ones [for whom] the state must furnish a lawyer. People with money who can hire the best lawyers are not on death rows. When I witnessed Robert's execution, I was looking directly at the injustice of the system — and I was appalled. A deep dedication came over me and I said, "Lord, help me wake America up." I was so hurt to know that I live in a country that's supposed to be a Christian country, yet so much injustice prevails; to know that men in high office are responsible for these injustices, and they are so corrupt themselves.

Reverend Brown walked out of the prison and embraced Rosella Williams. Her son was dead. His body had been destroyed, but not her memory of him. "They used my son," she told the media, "and they've abused my family."

She remained composed, her voice even and level, despite her grief. Her son had held strong in his death, and she would not dishonor his spirit by being less. Tears came later, but not there, not with the world watching. Then she made her final statement. "My son did not ask to be released from prison," she said, "but only to be given a life sentence where he could help others."

Williams's execution also deeply affected Sam Dalton.

I felt like I had been amputated when I heard that the execution had been carried out. It was a loss that I just couldn't believe. We got two votes from the pardon board, and while I think their decision was pre-ordained, we still got two votes. We simply made a straightforward presentation of the case to them. Now, Jesus Christ, what would have happened if that same presentation had been made to the jury? I can't help but believe that he would have persuaded at least one juror to vote for life — and that was all he needed.

Charles Kelly refused to accept the non-intent defense. "I never believed the shooting of my father was an accident," he said. "I will never believe it was an accident. I believe in the death penalty in certain kinds of cases. I have three sons — one twenty-two, one nineteen, and another small one — and if one of my sons did what Robert Wayne Williams did, I don't think I could support him in trying to avoid the death penalty."

After the Williams execution, Claude Pennington III received a three-year probated sentence as part of the plea agreement that his lawyer, Bryan Bush, had negotiated. U.S. District Court judge John Parker didn't believe Pennington was a trafficker but merely a user. "I hope you will utilize the time on probation and take advantage of the break this court has given you," the judge said. "You ought to face up to your personal responsibilities and rid yourself of the drug habit. I hope you will be able to assume the role of a productive member of society."

Then Glen D'Spain and Kraemer Diel faced the court. They entered guilty pleas contingent on agreements to continue their cooperation with federal authorities in the massive drug probes. Diel agreed to serve as a witness for the government in future criminal trials dealing with local cocaine trafficking.

Ossie Brown announced that he would ask Louisiana attorney general William Guste to investigate a perjury charge against Glen D'Spain in light of his previous testimony before a state grand jury that he knew nothing about cocaine. As required by law, Assistant U.S. Attorney Stanford Bardwell responded by asking the Louisiana secretary of state's office to certify Brown and Bourland as public officials. In January 2004, Assistant U.S. Attorney Richard Simmons announced that Marian Whitaker's attorney had reached an agreement with the U.S. attorney's office. They would defer her trial for twelve months. Part of the agreement required Whitaker to remain under the minimal supervision of the probation department of the federal court. She had become a witness against Brown.

"We have a subject that does not warrant felony prosecution," Bardwell explained, saying such arrangements are not unusual and that such a subject "probably would not go to jail if convicted on a first offense."

In February 1984, Glen D'Spain and Dr. Kraemer Diel appeared before Judge Parker for sentencing. He gave both men a one-year probated sentence for cocaine possession. Four days later, a federal grand jury indicted Ossie Brown and David Bourland, charging them with mail fraud, conspiracy to extort, and extorting $168,869.66 from James D'Spain. Brown faced an additional four counts of making false statements to a grand jury.

While the flamboyant district attorney was ultimately acquitted of the corruption charges, the scandal forced him from office and he was never able to resurrect his political career. His days of power and glory ended, and he became just another lawyer in Baton Rouge —

one who didn't enjoy any remarkable degree of success after his fall from political grace.

The murky waters of corruption and drug trafficking obscured the serious legal issues in Williams's case, just as Reverend Brown had indicated after Williams's death. I believe politics killed Williams then. I can formally put it on the record now.

Appendix A

Methods and Offenses

The sad, sorry history of capital punishment in all its cruel and painful chapters is a study in sadistic behavior. Here is a list, by no means comprehensive, of various execution methods used across history.

animal attacks (alligators, ants, crabs, crocodiles, dogs, lions, piranhas, rodents, scorpions, sharks, snakes, spiders, wolves, etc.)
boiling to death
breaking wheel
burial alive
burning
crucifixion
crushing

decapitation
dehydration
disembowelment
dismemberment
drawing and quartering
drowning
electrocution
explosives
firing squad
flaying
flinging
garrote

gassing
guillotine
hanging
immurement
impalement
iron maiden
lethal injection
marooning
pendulum blade

poisoning
sawing
scaphism (cooping up,
   daubed with honey, to
   be eaten by insects)
slow slicing
stabbing
starvation
stoning

And here is a list of offenses that have merited the death penalty here in the United States:

aiding a runaway slave
arson
burglary
concealing the birth or
  death of an infant
counterfeiting
criminal assault
desertion
espionage
forgery
horse stealing

kidnapping
piracy
rape
robbery
slave revolt
sodomy/bestiality
theft
train robbery
treason
witchcraft

Appendix B

Statistics

- Fifteen people have been executed since 1976 who did not directly kill anyone. They were convicted either as accomplices to a felony murder or for ordering a contract killing. Of their codefendants (the actual killers), seven were also executed, while six received life sentences. Two codefendants died and another committed suicide. One codefendant remains on death row.

- Some states impose the death penalty for nonmurder offenses. Nine states and the federal government have the death penalty for treason. Six states allow the death penalty for sexual offenses involving a minor, five states allow it for aggravated kidnapping, two states for drug trafficking, two states for aircraft hijacking, one state for placing a bomb near a bus terminal, one state (and the federal government) for espionage, and one state for aggravated assault committed by an incarcerated felon who is a repeat offender or is convicted of murder at the time of the new assault. Federal capital crimes also include large-scale drug trafficking and the targeting of principals in racketeering trials.

- As of January 1, 2008, California led the nation with the most condemned prisoners, 667, followed by Florida with 397 and Texas with 373. Of the thirty-five states with a death penalty, ten states had more than a hundred inmates on death row, ten states had fewer than ten, and only New Hampshire had none.

- As of January 1, 2008, the nation's death rows held 3,309 inmates. That number peaked in 2000 with 3,593.

- From 1977 through November 30, 2008, the inmates executed in America included 640 whites, 390 blacks, 79 Hispanics, and 24 designated as "other."

- For the same time period, the victims of those 1,135 executed killers included 1,326 whites, 242 blacks, 85 Hispanics, and 40 "other."

- Also in this period, 15 white offenders were executed for killing black victims, while 228 black offenders were executed for killing white victims.

- On November 30, 2008, Texas had the highest percentage of minorities on its death row, at 70 percent, followed by Pennsylvania at 69 percent.

- Between 1976 and 1998, the death penalty was imposed in only 2.2 percent of all the murder cases with known offenders.

- On January 1, 2008, men comprised 98.5 percent of the nation's death row population, while women made up 1.5 percent.

- At the end of 2006, the median education level of death row inmates was the eleventh grade. About 40 percent had a high school diploma or GED, 37 percent had an education level between the ninth and eleventh grades, 14 percent had an eighth-grade education or less, and 9 percent had some college.

- Also at the end of 2006, 54.8 percent of death row inmates had never been married, 20.6 percent were divorced or separated, 21.7 percent were married, and 3 percent were widowed.

- Of that same death row population, 8.4 percent had a prior homicide conviction, while 65.5 percent had a prior felony conviction.

- At the time of arrest, 50 percent of these inmates were aged 20–29, 11 percent were 19 or younger, and 1 percent were 55 or older. The average age at arrest was 28 years.

- Of these inmates, 33 percent were between 30 and 39 years of age, 59 percent were between ages 25 and 44, 1.6 percent were under the age of 25, and 1.5 percent were older than 65. As of 2005, 137 inmates on death row were 60 years old or older.

- In 2004, Alabama executed a 74-year-old man who suffered from dementia and colon and prostate cancer and was so weak that fellow inmates had to walk him to the shower and comb his hair.

- Attorneys for an 89-year-old condemned inmate, debilitated by deafness, arthritis, and heart disease, asked a federal court to declare unconstitutional the execution of inmates suffering from Alzheimer's disease, dementia, and other age-related infirmities.

- Between 1976 and 2006, 7,115 people were sentenced to death.

- Between 1973 and 2007, 162 death sentences were imposed on women in this country, of whom 105 were white, 43 black, 10 Hispanic, and 1 other.

- The women executed in the United States number 11 since 1976 and more than 40 over the past century. Of the 11 executed since 1976 (7 of them for murdering an intimate partner and/or their children), 9 were killed by lethal injection and 2 electrocuted. Oklahoma and Texas led these executions of women, with 3 each.

• Texas had not executed a woman in the twentieth century until it put Karla Faye Tucker to death on February 3, 1998.

• Oklahoma executed one woman in the twentieth century, Dora Wright on July 17, 1903, the century's first woman to be executed. Oklahoma didn't execute another woman until January 11, 2001, when it put Wanda Jean Allen to death.

• New York leads the nation with seven executions of women since 1900. The state no longer has a death penalty.

• At the end of 2007, 51 women sat on the nation's death rows, the youngest 23 years old and the oldest 73.

• In August 2007, the Pew Research Center reported that 62 percent of Americans support the death penalty. Support for the death penalty reached its peak in 1994, when 80 percent of the American public endorsed it. Between 1900 and 1940 support for the death penalty ranged from 9 percent to 42 percent. Its support began to increase in 1950, and since the 1960s has never fallen below 50 percent.

• At the end of 2007, 55 Florida inmates had been on that state's death row for 25 years and one had been there for 33 years.

• From 1978 through March 2008, Maryland spent at least $37.2 million for each of the five executions it carried out.

• The *Dallas Morning News* in March 1992 reported that a death penalty case cost Texas taxpayers three times as much as it would cost to keep a noncapital inmate incarcerated at the highest security level for forty years.

• In March 2008, retired Orange County Superior Court judge Donald McCartin, who sentenced nine men to death and saw every sentence overturned, pointed out that California has executed only thirteen inmates in thirty years. He also said that it costs ten times as much to kill an inmate as it would to incarcerate him for life.

- The *New York Times* reported in December 2004 that California spent $90 million annually above and beyond ordinary justice system costs in capital cases.

- In March 2005, the *Los Angeles Times* reported that California spent $114 million more annually to maintain the death penalty system than keeping convicts locked up for life.

- The Washington State Bar Association estimated in 2006 that it cost approximately $470,000 more in prosecution and defense costs to try a capital murder case than a noncapital murder case, with an additional $40,000 to $70,000 in costs for court personnel. On direct appeal in a death penalty case, it cost an average of $100,000 more in a capital than a noncapital case. Personal restraint petitions filed on behalf of death row inmates cost an average of $137,000 in public defense funds.

- New Jersey taxpayers paid $253 million between 1983 and 2006 to maintain the death penalty, according to a New Jersey Policy Perspectives report. Between 1982 and 2006, 197 capital trials in that state resulted in 60 death sentences, 50 of which were reversed on appeal. New Jersey abolished the death penalty in 2007.

- The *Palm Beach Post* reported in 2000 that Florida would save $51 million a year by punishing murderers with life without parole.

- Between 1639 and 2006, 464 Native Americans were executed in the United States. Since 1976, 15 Native Americans have been executed, and in 2006 there were 39 Native Americans on state and federal death rows.

- China abolished the death penalty briefly between 747

and 759. Grand Duke Leopold II, the future emperor of Austria, banned capital punishment in Tuscany in 1786. The Roman Republic banned the death penalty in 1849. Venezuela did the same in 1863, as did San Marino in 1865. Portugal abolished capital punishment in 1867 for ordinary crimes, and absolutely in 1976. France banned the death penalty in 1981, Australia in 1985, Canada and the United Kingdom in 1998.

- The state of Michigan abolished the death penalty in 1847.
- At the moment, fourteen other states and the District of Columbia also ban capital punishment.

Statistics courtesy of the
Death Penalty Information Center
www.deathpenaltyinfo.org

Acknowledgments

Portions of four chapters of this book previously appeared in the *Angolite*, the award-winning newsmagazine at the Louisiana State Penitentiary, where Billy was a staff writer, associate editor, and coeditor for nine years. He is grateful to former warden Ross Maggio and Assistant Warden Peggi Gresham for giving him the opportunity to join the publication.

Virtually all the statistics concerning the death penalty in this book come from the Death Penalty Information Center, an invaluable resource for anyone interested in capital punishment.

We also acknowledge the Gulf Region Advocacy Center in Harris County and the Texas Coalition Against the Death Penalty for their fine work against the death penalty.

We must give special acknowledgment to John T. Floyd, the Houston criminal defense attorney who hired Billy as his senior paralegal in March 2007. His Web site, www.johntfloyd.com, provides Billy with an opportunity to join with Mr. Floyd on joint literary efforts about legal and criminal justice issues.

Index